life
messages

life

messages

Inspiration for the Woman's

Spirit

Josephine Carlton

**Andrews McMeel
Publishing**

Kansas City

For information, write Andrews McMeel Publishing,
an Andrews McMeel Universal company, 4520 Main Street,
Kansas City, Missouri 64111.

02 03 04 05 06 QUF 10 9 8 7 6 5 4 3 2 1

Library of Congress Cataloging-in-Publication Data
Carlton, Josephine.
Life messages : inspiration for the women's spirit / Josephine Carlton.
     p. cm.
ISBN 0-7407-0023-5
  1. Women—Conduct of life. I. Title.
BJ1610 .C35 2002
158.1'2'082—dc21

                                                          2001053712

Book design by Holly Camerlinck

To the spirit of my loving mother,
whose memory is immortalized in my heart.

Contents

Hopi Prayer

Do not stand at my grave and weep.
I am not there, I do not sleep.

I am a thousand winds that blow,
I am the diamond glints on snow.
I am the sunlight on the ripened grain,
I am the gentle Autumn rain.

When you awaken in the morning hush,
I am the swift uplifting rush of quiet birds in circled flight.
I am the soft stars that shine at night.

Do not stand at my grave and cry: I am not there, I did not die.

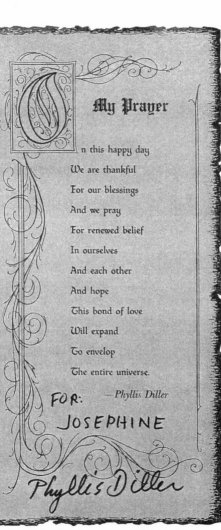

My Prayer

On this happy day

We are thankful

For our blessings

And we pray

For renewed belief

In ourselves

And each other

And hope

This bond of love

Will expand

To envelop

The entire universe.

— Phyllis Diller

FOR:

JOSEPHINE

Phyllis Diller

Introduction

Life Messages: Inspiration for the Woman's Spirit is the outcome of a complex, five-year process of evolution during which the book took on a life of its own. Originally the idea resulted from my own divorce experience, as a catharsis, perhaps, following the loss of a childhood sweetheart, best friend, husband of twenty-four years, and father of my three magical children. In the post-traumatic stress from this loss, I felt compelled to write a book to help other women survive a similar crisis. Soon, however, the scope of my exploration expanded until it embraced nearly every aspect of women's lives.

I began thinking about notable women, women of accomplishment who had undergone their own hardships, many of them greater than my own, and yet prevailed. I marveled at their strength and resiliency. What are the underlying reasons why some women prevail and others become victims? What are the sources of support, motivation, and belief in oneself that enable some women not only to survive, but to thrive? When did these women first feel they were in control of their own destinies? What roles were played in their life stories by other people, by chance and luck, by faith, by intuition? What messages might these women want to share that could comfort, challenge, and inspire other women?

I realized finally that my idea was about all kinds of women, not only the famous. I wanted to listen to women of many backgrounds, women from varying circumstances and all walks of life.

There were many more incarnations and reincarnations of this book before its essence came to fruition. Ultimately I settled on twelve broad areas of exploration, represented by the chapters in this book. Within each area, the women with whom I spoke contributed their memories, their reflections, their questions and struggles, and their wisdom. Along the way, they came to share in my personal journey of discovery. Our conversations elicited many moments of insight, much laughter, and not a few tears.

If there is a single overarching theme in this book, it is that each and every one of us has something wonderful to offer. All of us are exceptional in some respect. The challenge is to have our epiphany, to find out how to utilize our uniqueness not only for ourselves, but for others. In giving back to the world in which we live, we will no longer question the meaning of life or drown in our sorrows, but instead become strong, vital, and fulfilled. And like this book itself, the sum of our contributions will be greater than the parts.

Life Messages is an offering, not only my own, but more importantly an offering from the twenty-four women whose words and thoughts it contains. In it you will read how these remarkable women have struggled with many kinds of pain and adversity, risen above their difficulties, and found profound joy as they have followed their bliss. It is my hope that this book will inspire you to appreciate your own uniqueness, to revel in your personal journey, and to discover how your life can affect the world.

I know you will be inspired as I am by these fascinating life messages from truly incredible women. Now that the book is complete, I find myself reflecting upon these passages to guide my daily existence. The material gathered here has created a language of its own, one that speaks to inspire the spirit of women.

I want to thank each and every one of these women for contributing their time, their stories, and their passion to this collaborative endeavor of love. Bless all of you. May you continue to share the magic of your spirit.

Josephine Carlton

Chapter 1

Beginnings and Gaining Control of Your Life

When I was younger I was always trying to stop the bad times from coming. I resisted the bad times. Now I'm totally relaxed, totally open to whatever comes, the bad or the good, because what I have discovered is that I'm perfectly able to take it. Whatever happens, I can take it.

Isabel Allende

Many times I have pondered what determines the paths of life that we choose to follow. It seems to me that our vision of ourselves depends upon finding our gift to give to the world. When we have our epiphany and chart our individual destinies by making choices, we find the meaning and relevance of our lives. Our lives belong to us, and only we can adequately and ultimately determine what is right for us.

Determining our fate is a huge task not to be taken lightly. We only have one chance, one life, and we need to choose wisely. Yet, as the reflections of the women in this chapter show, our choosing is a journey, not a destination. When I asked these women about their beginnings, the moment when they began to grow into themselves and take charge of their lives, some immediately called to mind experiences in childhood or young adolescence, but others spoke of transformative events that happened much later in life, and are still happening. For them, mistakes, obstacles, and failures are all part of the process, guiding them in the right direction by eliminating the wrong choices.

As I listened to these women describe how they found confidence in their own powers and ability to direct their lives, it was this need to be constantly alert to our opportunities—the gifts that life offers us—that most struck me. Often enough those gifts come disguised; it is up to us to recognize and take advantage of them.

Isabel Allende

Author

My life has been about having a lot of success and happiness at a certain point, and then falling into an abyss and having great failures and losses. These ups and downs have been so notorious, so obvious in my life that I'm always *expecting* it.

At one time, for example, I thought that if I couldn't make enough money to support my family, it would be the end of it. It would be *awful!* But I've been so poor so many times and I've survived. I know now that even if I lose everything and become as poor as I was before, I can always start again . . . I thought that if something happened to any of my children I could not take it. I had to take a year off when my daughter was in a coma, and to grieve her death. And I have survived. So I know that I can take that, too. When I was younger I would say "If my mother died"—I have been very, very close to my mother, she's the strongest influence in my life—"I would die if she died." Now I know that not only will I not die, but I will be able to hold her, as I held my daughter. And I'm going to suffer *horribly* and it's okay because the suffering is as important in my life as the joy. The good times are as important as the bad times. In a way, I can't have one and not the other.

This is something very recent, but I think I have come to terms with all this after my daughter died. In the last five years I have developed a sort of detachment. It's not indifference, because I'm still as passionate about the same causes I believed in when I was young. I'm still a feminist, I'm still passionately involved in politics in the community. I love my writing, my work, my family. But I'm detached at the same time in the sense that I know *everything is temporary* and everything passes and goes, and it's okay. This is the nature of life. Everything dies. Even the storms change and die, so why not my daughter? The fact that it happened too early, that it happened in sort of an unnatural way— she died before I did, which would have been the natural order of things—doesn't mean much really. We are marked by the sign of fragility. This is what we are . . .

So it has been my karma, to lose everything and instead obtain things that I never aimed for.

Lynn Woolsey
Congresswoman

It's very clear to me that I've had to direct my life since I was a very tiny child and that I had choices as a little girl—either wallowing in a situation where I wasn't going to be very well taken care of, or taking charge myself. I really became big sister of my older sister and a surrogate mother to the family because that was necessary. But I still had a good time and never did any of these things without enjoying my life. So I learned very young to make the best of things and to enjoy life and have a good time. Part of that was about being able to work with people and live with people and do the best you can.

Carmel Greenwood
Entrepreneur

I was born in Western Australia. My father was a gold miner. In the beginning I grew up with the aborigines and went to school. It was a little like Arizona . . .

I had a vision when I was twelve. I saw Hong Kong and Athens, and I didn't know what they were at the time. But I knew that I wouldn't have the same life as my mother. She worked very hard and was the wife of a gold miner and yet it was very hard for her to give us food and stuff. I knew I wasn't going to have a life like that.

So, I left home at fifteen and went to Perth, the capital city in Western Australia, which is like San Francisco is to America. I worked as a secretary, I went to secretarial college, and I also worked in the Hamburger King at night because I wanted to leave Australia. I left on my eighteenth birthday and found myself on a ship bound for Athens! I arrived there and traveled around Europe. I was an au pair girl in Germany. I went to London and worked there for a year, and then I found myself on a ship going from Italy to Hong Kong. I was going there for a two-week holiday, but I ended up staying for twenty-seven years.

In Hong Kong I got offered a job and then I was asked by my husband to marry him. He was a policeman in Hong Kong. He was tall, handsome, good looking. When I married him I realized that actually I was replaying my mother's life. He was ten years older than I, as my father was to my mother. And he drank quite a lot of alcohol. I thought, "Well, I'll change him. When I have children, he'll change." But guess what? It got worse. So I had two children, a boy and a girl, and I lived with him for fifteen years. But after ten years I realized that it was not going to work. He was drinking, and at times he'd be very jovial and happy, then he'd be like Jekyll and Hyde. So we never knew what to expect. As his wife, I was expected to go to functions. He was then becoming an assistant commissioner of police in the Royal Hong Kong Police Force, so I had to go to dinners and play the "good wife." I was too afraid to leave him because I didn't think I could survive on my own. I realize now that that was just fear holding me back. When I look back now, it's so funny because what I've accomplished is a million times more than he ever did. But at the time it was very real . . .

Then I started planning to raise my self-esteem. I taught scuba diving and became a national scuba diving instructor. And I went to Toastmaster's. I learned to talk and how to promote myself and talk about myself. Before that I was afraid. I was really shy and withdrawn; afraid to talk to anyone . . .

Madeleine Albright
Former Secretary of State

My interest in international affairs began at an early age. My father was a Czech diplomat. By the time I was eleven, I had lived in five countries and knew four languages. In my parents' home we talked about international relations all the time, the way some families talk about sports or other things around the dinner table. As a child, living in so many foreign countries made it easier for me to adjust to different situations and to make friends, the essential skills of diplomacy. My mother always taught me to be open and friendly with new people. She said I could learn a lot from them, and she was right.

Rosie Casals
Professional athlete

I started playing tennis when I was about eight and a half, nine years old. My dad got me started. I used to sit by the window when he used to go off on the weekends to play out at Golden Gate Park.

Finally I convinced him to take me. I used to bug him to let me hit the tennis ball. Finally one day he realized that I was very, very serious about wanting to learn how to play. When I finally got on the court and showed him what I could do, he couldn't believe that I could hit the ball.

That was the beginning of a love affair with the game, and something that was very exciting to me, coming from the wrong side of the tracks. Tennis wasn't one of the games that we played outside. It was rather football, baseball.

I was in grammar school at that time, and I had a very special teacher I still keep in touch with. Her name is Lucy Paxton. She used to belong to the California Tennis Club, which is a very posh club in San Francisco. She kept saying, "When you get a little better, I will take you to the California Tennis Club . . ."

I did manage to go to the California Tennis Club. I played with my teacher. She likes to tell the story that all she saw was *bing bang*, and she could never hit the ball back because I was so good. She couldn't believe it. She encouraged me to continue playing, although I didn't need very much encouragement, because I knew that's what I wanted to do.

Naturally, during that time, we never knew anything about professional tennis or money, or what was going to happen to the game ten years, fifteen years from then. So I played because I loved it, and it was also a way that coming from the wrong side of the tracks—I would play in this group called the Whiteman Cup. We'd play every Monday and Friday. All the kids would show up in their Cadillacs and their white tennis skirts looking very prim and proper. And we didn't have that much money to spend on tennis clothes and things like that. So I think probably my way of getting back at them was that I was better.

And as I started to play junior tournaments, I started beating all of them, and became number one in my age group. So I think for me, it was a great way of feeling confident, and establishing myself, and saying, "Well, okay, I may not have all the things that you have, but I have something you don't have. And I'm good at what I do."

I think that it was very important to have that feeling, because I see people that don't have as much as others, or are not as confident, but if they're good at something, it really does help them learn about themselves and build up their confidence, and have a desire for something more. Tennis definitely gave me that.

Leslie Young
Ballet soloist

I started ballet when I was four years old. It actually wasn't my choice. My mom decided to start me for the summer. I was a little chubby and not necessarily coordinated. She thought this would be a good thing — ballet would help give me a bit of grace, a bit of coordination for my future, and I would feel good about myself and just stand up straight, I guess.

As years progressed I also studied the violin and the piano, and at some point my parents said, "Let's make a choice of what you want to do. We can't do all of these." So I guess that would be one of my first efforts to take control of my life. I was presented with a choice. I continued with all three for a little while, and slowly ballet was the one that I decided on. And I think it's because it's the one that I loved the most . . . Then and now, although I think I would describe it better now, I liked the challenge of the steps, of the physicality of it all. I loved the discipline. You don't think kids really like discipline, but they do—boundaries. For me, then and now, I loved having boundaries and finding my freedom in those boundaries.

Along with that comes the creativity, and because I'm not an extroverted person, I could find a voice, an expression I didn't have to say out loud. I didn't have to yell with my voice. When you dance, you can stay quiet. But you are speaking in another language and telling stories, expressing emotion.

Elizabeth Colton

Entrepreneur

After college I moved out to California, and I started getting involved in politics basically because I could vote. Somehow the enormity of being able to vote for who was going to be the president of the United States was very impressive to me, and I started becoming involved in political campaigns. Through that I met some other people in campaigns and I started working full-time in campaigns, first as a volunteer and later on as a paid staff person. I found that helping to influence who was elected to office was a good way to affect what was happening in the world. It was a big change you could make. I always wanted to make changes on a high level. It wasn't good enough for me to work one on one with somebody, although that's important work that people do and I don't disparage it in any way. But for me, I always felt like I wanted to change lots of things in the big picture. So I started working in politics.

Laurel Burch

Artist

I think one of the most profound things that I remember that really influenced my life and my ability—when I became aware that I could take circumstances over which I assumed that I had no control and influence the result—was in discovering when I was thirteen that I had a bone disease. It was the first time that I was aware of something intense and profound that would have an impact on me. I was most likely going to have this condition for my whole life. I didn't have a real sense of what that meant, but I did know that it had an impact on me right at that moment and the way that I experienced my life—I mean in the sense of being very fragile, very vulnerable, very separate from other young people, or any age of people.

I remember making the decision consciously that the way that I could really embrace it was to have it be a special thing instead of being something that was a negative thing. The way that I embraced it was to say that it was something unique and special and that while I couldn't control the fact that I had this condition, I could control the way that I felt about it and the way that I turned it into something that could be a positive thing. So on one hand I was very secretive about it. I felt ashamed of it and I felt different, but in the relationship between me and myself, on a very private level, it was something that I had come to terms with by feeling that it was special.

So I had this viewpoint of life that ultimately, as I got older, became the source of a lot of my strength: that I was isolated and special, vulnerable, and strong. I mean really all of those, the polarity of all those things had a tremendous impact on my life in a lot of ways. I don't remember anything as profound as that realization.

Nancy Currie

Astronaut

I think I was somewhat fortunate in that from the time I could walk I wanted to fly. At that point it was the early sixties, and little girls didn't really grow up to be pilots back then. But nobody really told me that, and so nobody squelched that desire in me. I'm very fortunate that I had teachers and family that were real supportive at that time, who never said, "Hey, that's a closed door, you can't go through it . . ."

Luckily, the military opened up flying opportunities to women in the mid-seventies, just about the time I was graduating from high school. And so I was able to go through college, go right into the military.

When I was in flight school in the military, something happened early on that I think was a significant change: There was an aircraft accident that killed the people that I flew with every day. And it was just kind of a fluke that I was not in the aircraft. I was flying with another set of crew members that day, and actually flying beside that aircraft, and watched it all happen. Obviously that's a real down period of your life, but I tried to become very introspective about it and say, "Hey, I was spared, I'm going to make a difference." That's why I shifted my life from medicine—my initial degree was in biology, and I was more geared toward preventive medicine and that kind of thing—toward safety and safety engineering, to prevent exactly the kind of accident that had occurred.

At any time in my life when I've thought, "Hey, this is difficult"—finishing my PhD when I was in my thirties would fall into that category, especially since I was doing it at night—I would always think, "Well, at least I've got that opportunity. I have that opportunity that these other folks never got a chance to have."

Rabbi Stacy Friedman
Rabbi

I knew from a young age that I wanted to be a rabbi. I knew when I was a young teenager that was what I wanted to do. I decided at the time that was the path I was going to pursue. So it was really an example of taking control of my life and directing my life even though it was something that I rebelled against. I took paths away from it and kept coming back to it . . .

I grew up in New York and then when I was twelve moved to Salt Lake City with my family. So I was swimming upstream against a pool that was very different for me, and I guess I was very different from everybody else in my surroundings. At that time, too, being involved in the Jewish community and doing what I do was very different.

I remember at the time I said before my congregation that I wanted to be a rabbi. Maybe there were five women rabbis in the country at the time. I didn't even know that women could be rabbis, but I'm one of three daughters, so from an early age I felt girls could do everything and anything. So taking control of my life was always something that was very natural.

Valerie Coleman Morris
Anchorwoman/TV personality

I start with the fact that I was born into a family that really knew what it meant to have a nuclear family, because it was oftentimes just my father and mother and me in foreign countries. My dad was in the Air Force. So, as someone who was born into an Air Force family and didn't have a sibling until I was eleven years old, the nuclear family took on even greater importance for me. All of my ups and downs were mitigated by my parents' attempts to make sure I was as normal as possible in the midst of times and circumstances where I wasn't experiencing on a daily basis the racism that we were facing in the United States. But I was coming back to this country every three to five years, so they wanted me fortified and ready to face what it was going to be like to be black in America versus being black in Europe.

I didn't really know ups and downs until I experienced them in my sophomore year of high school. That's when we came back to the States and I was the only black student in my school. Actually to me it was very normal because I didn't have anything to compare it with. But my awareness was growing of the various forms of discrimination, not just because of color, but also in the form of the city people thinking that those of us on the Air Force base were problematic people. We weren't necessarily welcomed by the community lock, stock, and barrel, and that was really hard because you then were identified as "kids from the base." So you were still a bit of an outsider because you lived in an environment that was a community in and of itself.

The point of the story is that diversity for me was always a journey, not a destination point, because I was always the one that was diversifying the mix. Ups and downs were things that I just expected, because until I could effect some kind of a change in the circumstance in which I was, things would remain as they always had been. So I kind of viewed life for me as, I was a catalyst for change. How's that for parents putting a great spin on what could have been a horrible experience?

Sylvia Boorstein
Author/Educator/Lecturer

I actually feel that my life is a gift and I didn't have ups and downs or even zigs and zags. I had a very warm extended family, and I was an only child. It was very pleasant in a Jewish family even though those were dreadful years for Jews in this country and in the world because of anti-Semitism and the impending Holocaust in the 1940s in Europe.

My family's Judaism was traditional and at the same time progressive; my whole life is paradoxical. It was a traditional family in the sense that we were traditionally observant without being tight, worried, or frightened about it. That has a lot to do with why I love being a Jew so much. We lived in a committed Jewish cultural context with calendar and dietary observance. It wasn't a complication. We lived in Brooklyn, and everybody around us did the same things.

I graduated college with a degree in chemistry and mathematics and married at the end of my junior year. I married a predictable person for me to marry—a man five years older than myself who had just graduated from medical school, also a Jew.

I met my husband when I was fifteen years old. I didn't have that many boyfriends before him. I married him when I was eighteen, and I have the great, good fortune to still be married to him. Some of it is diligence, but mostly it is great, good fortune because we were really too young to have anything other than an instinctive sense that this was a good match.

My husband became a psychiatrist. My interest in what he was doing outweighed my interest in chemistry and mathematics, so I went back to school when I was twenty-eight and got a master's degree in social welfare. I've worked with clients, at social agencies, I taught psychology in junior colleges, I went back and got a doctorate in psychology and learned Hatha Yoga as a discipline. I then taught it in addition to teaching psychology for fifteen years in a local junior college. I became very interested in how the mind and the body operate together and how keeping your attention focused created certain, more peaceful mind states. In the 1970s, when everyone else was getting interested in meditation and transformation, I also got interested. In fact, my husband's spiritual adventures got me to try a number of things. It's not a feminist thing to say. But the fact is that I had four children and a very full career as a psychotherapist, and I was a tremendous activist in the peace movement in the Vietnam times and afterward. So I really think that those spiritual needs that I had at the time were met through social activism and through working as a psychotherapist.

Then came along all of these meditation practices. I went to a mindfulness retreat, which is a retreat in Theravada Buddhist tradition taught by Americans in English, contemporaries of mind younger than I. I just fell in love with it. The lesson is so straightforward and clear. Life is what it is.

Sometimes it's difficult and sometimes it's a joy. Our experience of life, in that we experience it as suffering or as a thrilling life, depends on the mind state that we bring to our experience, and we can cultivate that spaciousness of mind that lives through the pain and appreciates the joy, and do it with wisdom. That was such a compelling teaching that I never left.

Over the last twenty-three years I've been a practitioner and somewhere along the line became a teacher of mindfulness, which is the principal teaching of paying attention to what the Buddha taught, and that's a loving kindness. The parallel teaching is that of cultivating a steadfast goodwill in the heart. This really is a reflection of the understanding that when we are not frightened, we are, just by virtue of being human beings, connected to each other with loving kindness.

That's a very long answer, but that's what I did with my life. I'm sixty-three years old.

Reverend Veronica Goines

Presbyterian pastor

For me, some of the biggest turning or transitional points came out of relationship changes, beginning with my first marriage . . . The conclusion of the marriage was a time of taking stock in my life. I realized that I didn't really have any goals for myself. My entire goals for my life were wrapped into this marriage. I think I went to college just with the thought of being a better educated mother and wife and not so much with the intent of ever becoming any kind of professional person. It wasn't because I didn't think I had gifts, it was because for me relationship has always been at the center of who I am. At that time I hadn't explored anything beyond that.

So at the point that the marriage had fallen apart, it forced me to make some tough decisions in my own life. That's where a lot of my beginning started in terms of exploring possibilities for myself. I went to libraries and talked to career counselors and so forth. When I did all this research, what I came up with was the field of graphic design, which my bachelor's degree was in—fine arts. I knew that I wasn't going to make it as a fine artist, so that began this turning point in my life where I actually began to see myself. I could visualize myself as this professional person in this graphic arts field. That's exactly what happened not too long after that.

Irene Zisblatt Zeigelstein
Holocaust survivor

Until I was twelve, thirteen years old, I lived in a resort town in the mountains, in Hungary. My life up until the Nazi regime was very normal, very happy. I had a large family; there were six siblings, grandparents on both sides, parents, cousins, aunts, uncles galore, and we were only about sixty-three Jewish families in town. We were 178 families all together, so it was just a little bigger than a village. But it was a resort town, and people from all over the country and out of the country came to us because my father was part owner of a spa.

My non-Jewish friends and Jewish friends, we were like one family. There was no difference because we were Jewish. We shared our lives until the Nazis came in when Hungary started to collaborate with the Nazis. When I was nine years old, I was thrown out of my school because I was Jewish. That's when things started to happen big time. I was very devastated for being who I was. I could not understand why I had to be treated differently all of a sudden, by my friends, by my neighbors. Being Jewish didn't make any difference yesterday, and today I am just not the same person in their eyes. There was a lot of hatred I noticed. I could not understand. I asked questions. My parents wouldn't answer my questions, and what else can I tell you?

Marti McMahon

Entrepreneur

I can remember way back when I was a child. I was very entrepreneurial and started my first business when I was seven. My family was very poor. We lived in a two-room apartment in Chicago, having moved here from El Salvador. My mother, who was extremely creative, taught me how to make tissue flowers out of Kleenex. And I made those and would go door-to-door selling them for twenty-five cents. That was my first business, and I guess that every time I would turn a corner I would think of something—"Oh, wow! There's something there that could be a business." I don't know whether entrepreneurs are just born. I think it so happened for me.

Jo Hanson

Artist/Environmentalist

I thought about it, and it seemed to me that my first effort to take charge of my life was being born. Growing up is sort of an ongoing effort to take control of your life. I had very little success, but something must have happened, because at about age twelve I announced that I was not going to church anymore. I guess my mother and father had got religion at some point and not only did they go to church on Sunday, they went on Wednesday night too. They dragged me to all of these things as a small child. I think church might be more appealing now, but certainly it was not appealing to me at the time and those wooden benches were not inviting. The only relief was a couple of stained glass windows that I can still see.

The church was called First Christian. This was in southern Illinois, and there was a strong element of fundamentalism in that area. At that time it was sinful to wear lipstick, to dance, and obviously to smoke or take a drink, and a lot of other things that are done routinely.

I suffered through this year after year after year. At age twelve I announced that I did not believe all of this and that I had read about evolution or heard about it and I was not going to go to church and Sunday school anymore.

It still surprises me that I got by with it, but I guess I was a very difficult child. It wasn't that I was difficult in a positive way, because I've always felt guilty about what I did, but I also felt I just couldn't go along with what was being pushed at me. The thing I heard most commonly was "Little girls don't do that," and that applied to almost everything I wanted to do. The other thing was "What's wrong with you? What will the neighbors think?"

So I was taking in a rather difficult self-image, and it took me a long time to realize that the neighbors weren't thinking about me all the time and mainly weren't judging me and if they were, maybe they liked what I was doing.

That took a lot of time and doing. There were no times except for this twelve-year-old all-out rebellion when I could say specifically how I was taking charge of my life.

Mary Bitterman
President/CEO, public television

I was born and raised in San Jose, in the valley of heart's delight, the youngest of three children, the two older siblings being brothers. I was raised in a household with four grandparents, so a knowledge and respect for older people developed at a very, very early age. Because of four grandparents and three children in a household, everyone had responsibilities, and I think directing my life and taking control of my life was done in a sense of recognizing both rights and responsibilities. I think from a very early age I recognized that what perhaps some children saw as desirable, always being the center of attention, simply wasn't possible in our household. And it was probably not a terrible phase to have never had. Because I think the important thing is for all of us to contribute to the success of one another, and not need to be at the center of everyone's attention and activity.

I worked from the time I was twelve in summer jobs and things, picking plums initially, and then doing other jobs and working through college and graduate school. I always had a number of responsibilities, and pretty much tended to them. I don't remember that there were huge parts of my very early life in which there wasn't a certain amount of order. I think part of that is, if you have four elderly people in the household, two of whom are invalids, you can't not be home at a certain time to help get dinner. And you can't not do a thing, because everyone was expected to fulfill certain responsibilities, to have things run in a way in which every member of the family could function.

Sister Mary Neill
Nun/Author/Educator

I'm sixty-six years old. I will have been in religious life next year for fifty years. I was seventeen years old when I entered. As I look back on my life, I often say that I was seventeen going on three when I entered, and what has kept me in religious life is a very different thing than what brought me to it. Part of my inner journey is why in the world would a person, a woman, come into a life not in giving birth to others but, in a way, caretaking others. This has been a great mystery to me . . .

Sometimes when I thought about when I first became a nun, I'd say it was when I was four years old under the trees in Colorado. I was very, very happy and I thought at that time—I felt very deeply in my body—that I was not to belong to anybody, that there would never be anyone there for me. So there was this sense of being an orphan, and entering the religious life had that sense that I was not to have a husband, I was not to have children, that I was to be somehow for the world.

I look back and think, what a proud and arrogant thing, why would anyone feel called to do that? And so the last fifty years I've had various relationships to this call, looked at the pathology of it—you know, what was it about marriage I experienced as a child, that I thought marriage wouldn't be good? Since my degree was in religion and psychology, I had had a lot of therapy of every kind that you would want, but it is a profound mystery to me . . .

One of my favorite quotes is "If we are to trust anything at all, we're to trust what's been given us." So I remain a Catholic because I was born in a Catholic womb. The Catholicism in my mother was intense as a convert, and I've been through many stages of that Catholicism. Much I find very difficult, hard to believe in. A part of being a Roman Catholic nun is the education, the emancipation, the power that the women have—so much so that we've been investigated by the Pope as undermining the Church. I would say he's not entirely wrong, because my own life story has been to accept these roles, to trust them and then to live in contradiction to them, to rebel against them and find out "Well, now, now what's true for me?" Here is the collective myth about what is a nun. Here's my personal pathology about what's a nun. But here's the mystery of what's a nun.

When I was forty years old, I moved to Europe to get my doctorate. Because I entered so young, I think I went to find out was there really a nun inside me, or was it all external? I'm a pleaser and all that, so was there anything in me that was truly a nun? And when I was over there I found that there was. She wasn't a twenty-four-hour nun. She was a little tight hot spot of gravity in me. So there was validity for that, and I made my prayer to God at that time and said, "God, I don't know why I'm a nun, but if you don't want me to do this, if I can't keep myself alive, then give me a clear message."

When I came home, we had a meeting one time on the vows. One of the nuns who later became my best friend stood up and said, "You know, I don't know what 'poverty, chastity, and obedience' means, Sisters." Everyone gave a little gasp. And she said, "So I don't know what I vowed to you in that, but I know what my vow to you is now. I vow to keep myself alive." And something clicked in me, and I thought, that's all that God has asked of me is that I keep myself alive and how within these forms, which are tight and sometimes treacherous, how have I kept myself alive? How have they enabled me to keep myself alive?

Jeanne Rizzo

Entrepreneur

I grew up thinking that girls could only be nurses, mothers, secretaries, wives, or teachers. I chose nursing because I felt a tug at my compassion. I had life-threatening hepatitis when I was in grade school, and I think that inspired me to come to understanding the dark side. I felt a real dark side around that and felt inspired to take hold of my education. And I wanted to get out of the house. Nursing school afforded me the opportunity to leave home, get a scholarship, and not have to live in that home. So I left home right after high school and lived with friends and then went on to nursing school. I reestablished a relationship with my parents from that place of independence.

My father's advice to me was never depend on any man even though he required that of my mother. That became my mantra, that I wasn't going to do that. I was going to be independent and have my own income and not get married and have kids right away, which I didn't do. I went into psychiatric nursing and I was an administrator and a teacher of nursing.

What efforts did I use to take control of my life? I used my education and success in school, and I had my activism spurred by a situation when I was in school of the nurses' strike in 1965 in New York. The nurses went on strike for pay that would be equal to teachers, and I led the state student nurses in not crossing the picket lines. So that was my first taste of activism, that I could make a difference beyond my own world. It was important to me to understand that the world was bigger than just my own. So I think I got that in nursing school, and I felt tremendous energy in groups of people being political and being active in changing the world. So I think that commitment started then.

Chapter 2

Courage and Motivation

Yes, life has all of these other different facets to it, but you're
given a choice, and I choose consciously to see the beauty
and the richness in the lovely, wonderful things about life.
Everyone has that choice, and they can make that choice at
any time. So that's how I feel. Here we are and life is good.

Laurel Burch

I am fascinated by courageous pursuit of purpose. All the
women I spoke with are, in different ways, women of accomplishment.
Where did their motivation come from? Where did they get the
courage to do what they loved despite discouragements, failures, the
obstacles that life always throws in our way? Why did they persevere?

For these women, motivation, courage, and inspiration came variously from family, from concern for their children, from a sense of love
and compassion, or simply from necessity. Several did not claim courage

for themselves; they saw themselves as simply doing what they had to do, what their circumstances called for. Whether or not we call it courage, physical limitations, financial necessity, and oppression induced resourcefulness in these women. They developed other aspects within themselves such as their minds and imaginations to improve their circumstances. For me, perhaps their most inspiring message is: "I did it. You can, too."

Isabel Allende
Author

What gave me the courage to live my dreams? I didn't have any particular courage, I just coped. And if I had dreams, I wasn't doing things to fulfill the dreams. I was just coping. Raising kids, working to make a living. The most important thing was to make enough money to pay for their education, to give them a good life. So I worked all my life in several jobs just to give them a good life. This was essential for me, so I just coped with life.

If I had dreams, they were always postponed because they were not important. Other things were much more important—my responsibility as a mother, as a daughter, as a wife. All those things came first. And even now that I'm a grandmother and I have done so many things in my life, I don't think of my dreams. I think only of what I have to do to make life better for people around me and therefore for myself.

Lynn Woolsey
Congresswoman

I think one of the most important things for me is that if I'm interested in something I want to be part of it, and I want to be part in a very positive way whenever possible.

When I was in the ninth grade I was vice president of my girls' club, later on in life part of the women's movement and part of the environmental movement and a member of the city council. Each time these were issues that I was involved in and rather than just be in the back yapping about it, I wanted to be part of making things happen. I'm a perfectly okay teammate, but if nothing is happening I take charge. That goes way back to when I was four years old. If it wasn't happening I'd take charge because I wasn't going to let it go down the dumps.

One thing was comparing and knowing how I wasn't going to be. I had an absolutely beautiful mother. If she were living today, she would think that the reason President Clinton mentioned me in the State of the Union speech a few years ago was because he had a crush on me. She could not, in her lifetime, understand that men and women can know each other and work together. To her, a woman couldn't be respected for her accomplishments and brains. It had to be for what she looked like. That was sad for me, but I didn't want to be that way. Your looks last so long, but the rest of you lasts forever if you let it. I just wasn't going to be that way—narcissistic. I wasn't going to be there just for the social part of life. I wanted to be part of the soul of life.

I grew up with two older brothers. It was a good training ground to learn courage. I remember even when I was one or two, they used to roll me down this hill and I would fall out of my stroller. I've always had the courage to dust myself off and start all over again. I've realized that I have just this life and I'm going to live it to the full, no matter what it looks like.

Gretchen Dewitt
Public relations professional

I was probably motivated by Doris Day and Rock Hudson to fall in love and get married. Isn't that disgusting?

I grew up on innocent love stories and love movies. And I was very motivated to have a big love story. Money? When did money enter into the picture? Money still hasn't entered into the picture for me. I don't think about money. It's true. I don't think about saving it. I don't think about getting it. When I have it, I sort of spread it around like peanut butter or manure, thinking this is what's going to make everything else grow.

But I was never motivated by money, which has been an impracticality in some cases. When I got a divorce with two small children, the lawyer asked me what I'd like. And I said I'd like "out" and I'd like my children. So I didn't take anything. I didn't take the furniture from our home, I just walked out. So money has not ever been a motivating factor in my life.

I think for most people who decide to work because they love what they'll be doing, they don't have to think ultimately of money as a goal. They have the money coming as a result of putting their love and energy into what they're doing. And I think it's automatic that they are much happier people as well. They are successful people. People who love what they are doing are successful. And the money comes in as a natural aftereffect of working hard and loving it, being inspired about work.

Alice Waters
Restaurateur/Author/Educator

I think I was very much in the spirit of what was going on during the Free Speech Movement, in Berkeley and around the country. I just felt like, doors opened up at that point, and everyone felt as if he could accomplish whatever he wanted to do. Or she wanted to do. And if it was good, people would come.

It was that whole counterculture movement that gave me the courage or the support that I needed to feel like I could open a restaurant—on ten thousand dollars. So, it was naïveté, I think there was a lot of naïveté, and just a feeling in the air that we could change the world and it was possible to do things that people thought were impossible. And that's a great feeling.

I just think I had good timing. Very good timing. Timing is terribly important.

Madeleine Albright
Former Secretary of State

I could not say to you that it had always been my ambition to be Secretary of State of the United States. Frankly, I did not think it was possible. I arrived in America when I was eleven years old. My family came here to escape Communism and to find freedom, and we did. My ambition at that time was only to speak English well, please my parents, study hard, and grow up to be an American.

My appointment as Secretary of State does show the incredible opportunity in this country . . . I was also our representative in New York at the United Nations and found that world was a great challenge and an honor. Whatever gender one is, that is not the point of it. The point is to have the opportunity of representing the United States.

When I appear in public or walk along the street, people rush up to me. They don't say Madam Secretary, they call me Madeleine. I think it is because people feel that a woman Secretary of State—this woman—is approachable, and they are transferring it somehow to demystifying foreign policy. They even say they're reading more about foreign policy these days. I think that's great.

I am fluent in French and Czech. I also have good speaking and reading abilities in Russian and Polish. My own life has convinced me of the value of language study. I have often explained that I learned my French in a Swiss boarding school where, if you couldn't speak properly, you wouldn't eat. Most people's motivations are not that urgent, of course. But the language skills do open all kinds of doors in one's personal and professional life, especially today. I believe that my ability to speak Russian was definitely an asset in building my relationship with the Russian Foreign Minister and President Yeltsin. I believe that others sense your respect for them and your honest desire for mutually beneficial results when you have taken the time to try to better understand them and their culture by learning their language—and it's never too late . . .

Leslie Young
Ballet soloist

I think everyone has something that they love to do. It's a matter of finding it. Even though you have ups and downs, if you truly love it, that's your golden thread that runs through every day . . .

I was blessed with finding it early. Ballet is not easy. There are a lot of physical restrictions and limitations and challenges and obstacles that you have to overcome. But there's always that glorious music supporting you, and your love for movement and expression. You don't necessarily have all those elements in each ballet, but you'll surely have one of them, and that keeps you going. It keeps me going.

Annelies Atchley
Educator/Artist

If you have it tough enough in life as a woman, you need to make a roof over your head. I was thrown out of the house at sixteen. I was grateful for just having a roof over my head. Just a roof so I didn't have to sleep under a tree. That makes you a different kind of person because you work all the time to survive. You don't ask anymore "What do I want?" or "What can I have?" You just do the best you can under the circumstances and let opportunities come at you that you grab because they're better than what you had before. So you're ultimately improving yourself because you're taking opportunities that come your way that are better than the situations you are in. So you're never looking for anything and you're basically surviving, but you're also open to all the opportunities that come because each little step is better than the one before . . .

So, when you look for men—I never looked for men because I had such a bad experience with my son's father, who left and I was all by myself and then I had to give my son away because he needed a family. I wasn't looking for a man to take care of me or make me a better person or represent my family background or give me a religious background or do financial things or be my companion. I didn't look for that. I wasn't looking for a companion because I was too busy doing my job the best I could.

So, when Bill came along, he was a nice person. He was older and probably not the most handsome, and he especially wasn't physically fit as I would have liked him to be, but he was a nice person, a kind person, and that I didn't have in my life. So I took the opportunity to go out to dinner, and when he said, "Could you stay over?" I said, "I don't want a boyfriend. I don't want to get involved right now, because that's how a teacher stays clean in this town."

So we went out, we went for walks, and I would rather talk to him because he was a kind person. I did go out for dinner with him, and it developed into a very deep friendship, and then I thought: "I want to be with this guy even if he doesn't want to be with me. It doesn't matter because I'm not that emotionally involved. If he wants a better woman, he can have one."

This whole thing grew deeper and deeper. Year after year it got deeper, and now he has cancer and some things we don't do anymore together, but the personal thing that we have together is deeper and deeper and deeper. I would have never had that had I looked for a man who would fit into what I wanted. So that's why I think I have such a relationship and I think that's also true in life. I have to do what the opportunity is to do.

Laurel Burch
Artist

My motivation and courage come from my legs breaking without my really doing anything. Mine broke when I was seven in midair. And then when I was eleven my leg broke in midair and then I fell when I was thirteen and broke it. So it was a series of those things happening and then realizing that there was something unusual going on.

The other thing that really influenced me was that I was able to kind of move in my imagination a lot and create my own reality because the circumstances were often too challenging, too painful, too difficult, too uncertain in terms of my fragility. So I could utilize my mind and my imagination, my innovation, my creativity, to have some control over my experience, and that became something that I chose to do as a real positive in my life . . .

I want to take things that could have a totally different outcome and contribute. I want to contribute joy and celebration and color and life and vibrancy and positive, beautiful, wonderful things . . . That is the beauty of creating. Yes, life has all of these other different facets to it, but you're given a choice, and I choose consciously to see the beauty and the richness in the lovely, wonderful things about life. Everyone has that choice, and they can make that choice at any time. So that's how I feel. Here we are and life is good.

Nancy Currie
Astronaut

The first thing you learn is that this profession is a very dangerous profession, and that's flying in general, not necessarily flying in space . . . I guess I'm pretty driven because I never want anything to be a result of my lack of knowledge of the situation, of my lack of skills in a situation.

There are certain things that can happen in aircraft or in the shuttle that are totally beyond your control. At that point you're along for the ride; essentially you're in God's hands. But there are opportunities to influence that through your skill, your knowledge, and so it changed my perspective on life to say that in anything I did I wanted to be the best I possibly could from a technical perspective.

Rabbi Stacy Friedman
Rabbi

I find that in terms of motivation and courage, the courage comes from not fighting destiny. I think that when we do things that we're meant to do, it's very natural. It's not that it's easy, but it's very natural to do. It gets hard when we fight it.

There were times when I fought it. I took a few years off after college and said, "I'm not going to go be a rabbi. I'm going to go do something else. I'll go get my MBA or I'll do this or I'll do something else, and I don't have to do that," and yet I kept coming back to it. I think our lives are really hard when we fight our destiny. The hardest thing to do is to open up to the truth that God has implanted in us. It's really hard to be centered in that truth. For me that's hard.

What motivated me were all of my compulsions and interests and my love of prayer and community and people and teaching and all that sort of thing. What gave me the courage to do that was, number one, the idea that I could do anything that I wanted to do, which I had from a young age, but also not fighting against it.

There were still things that I was afraid about that I'm still afraid of every day when I get out of bed. "Can I do this? Can I really do this?"

I remember when I was applying to rabbinical school because I wanted to do this for so long and then I thought—the first year is in Israel—I thought, "I'll just go to Israel because I love being in Israel and then I'll see what happens. I don't really have to stay." Then, before the end of the year, I said, "I'll just do another year and then I'll see what happens." The program is five years. So halfway through it I had this little crisis—I used to have them before finals all of the time—and I sat down with a professor of mine and said, "I don't know if I want to be a rabbi. I'm afraid of this and the commitment and the work and all this." He said, "Well, what do you do for fun?" I said, "I'm taking this Jewish meditation class and this Israeli dancing and . . ." He said, "It sounds like you want to be a rabbi."

So I think part of it is that no matter what we do, it's hard. There are difficult things, and I think that's where the courage takes place. I think women who stay home with their kids are really brave. It takes a lot of courage to do that. It takes a lot of courage to do what we do also. So I think we're all brave.

Sylvia Boorstein
Author/Educator/Lecturer

One of the things that has been interesting—my friend Mary Neill has been a nun since she was seventeen, and she's been tremendously inspiring to me. I said, "Look what affirmative action you do. Look how you knew what you wanted." Whereas I feel like everything has been a gift. I fell into my family and had the gift of a family that could have been patriarchal and wasn't. My father thought my mother was marvelous and thought that I was great in a culture that often did not respect women. My father took an extra job so that I could go to a women's college and in a tradition that didn't in those days especially educate women or include them in prayer services . . .

I feel like I walk between the waves or the raindrops in a certain way. My life has been graced. I met a man that I fell in love with when I was fifteen. I had four children who, thank God, are in good health. So I feel like my life has been carried along. I loved being a mother. It was a wonderful time in my life. I was eager to have those four children. I loved going to school to learn to be a psychologist, and I loved helping people psychologically. So each thing came along. I didn't feel like I had to get through certain hurdles.

Now, when I look at my life, I think, "My cup runneth over." I get to be teaching exactly what I want to teach, I get to be helpful, I get to teach mindfulness all over the place that's helpful to all kinds of people . . .

Everything that I've ever learned in my whole life and everything I've ever been is a part of what I'm doing. At no point did I make a plan to become it. It just happened.

Reverend Veronica Goines
Presbyterian pastor

I think I was motivated because I was forced to be. I didn't really have a whole lot of choice. I could have chosen not to do anything at all, but that wasn't who I was about either. I never had that kind of a role model. My mom went to work when I was five years old. She did domestic work when I was very young working for another family in Orange County or someplace a ways from where we lived. She got her AA degree in accounting, so she began to do jobs in accounting. She worked outside of the home and in the home, and so there was a different model that I had. It wasn't someone who just stayed home or expected someone to take care of her, although my dad certainly always provided for the family. So that was a part of what motivated me, my upbringing and my own environment or the environment that I came out of.

From there it was really being pushed and knowing that I wanted to model a lifestyle for my daughters as they were coming up. At the time of my separation I was actually seven months pregnant with my second daughter, so she wasn't even here yet. I just knew that I wanted her to come into a household where my children did not feel that they had some kind of second-class household because there wasn't a father present. I knew that I needed to acknowledge the absence but at the same time provide a wholesome, loving, and healthy environment for them. A lot of that inspired me to go on and pursue my own goals, which changed later down the road.

Irene Zisblatt Zeigelstein
Holocaust survivor

Teach your children tolerance and heal hatred. That is the truth of having a better world.

This is what the Holocaust was about. Hatred started the whole thing. Greed, hatred, all that stuff, and I think the women can help heal that. They can start with the children. I always said at thirteen children should learn all about the Holocaust, but I think today's children are mature enough at the age of eleven, twelve. So if women have children that age, they should encourage them to learn the history of the Holocaust, because they will learn values.

I have such a result when I speak in schools. I have to read you this. This is from a twelve-year-old child that has seen the movie *The Last Days*. You know *The Last Days*? Okay. Then right after the movie I spoke about my experience and the movie. Then they were asked to write about the day.

I am in the movie. There are five of us in the movie. We all have segments in the movie. Then we speak to these children around these segments. This child, she's not even Jewish, and she is a sixth grader, so she is twelve, right? This is what she writes.

"Last Thursday I was given a wonderful opportunity to see a documentary about the Holocaust. The movie that I saw touched me in many different ways. It made me realize how lucky I am to be learning about the Holocaust. The Holocaust is an extremely important lesson that everyone young and old should learn. It's not just a lesson on the horrible things the Jews in Europe and in the Middle East had suffered. It's a lesson about respecting others for who they are even if they are different."

This is what I'm teaching. This is what these kids get.

"I have had an understanding of the Holocaust for quite some time now, but it wasn't to the extent of what I have learned this year. In the past I knew that a group of people called the Nazis had murdered hundreds of people just because they were Jewish. But now my knowledge includes the true horrors of the Holocaust. I know now that millions of Jews were killed along with Poles, Czechs, homosexuals, and many others. I know that they were locked up in concentration camps, gassed to death in gas chambers, and starved to death just because they were different.

"This is a hard thing to understand for a teenager growing up in America today. But the movie brought it to life like few things have before. The movie wasn't just a scholar's telling people about the Holocaust. It was real people who had survived the Nazi torture and were telling their stories that makes things come to life.

"Before I saw the movie, I couldn't totally picture what happened not so long ago. But now I can . . . If everyone can realize just how cruel we can be to each other, our world would be rather peaceful and people would not be so disrespectful to each other.

"I think that the Nazis have proved two things. One is that ignorant people can be persuaded to believe anything even if it is false. The second is that if you teach others about horrible things that have happened in the past, then you are sure to prevent those things from happening again. As we teach future generations of the world about the Holocaust and to love one another, then the world will be a better place. I hope that everyone has an opportunity to learn what I have and to learn the lessons the Holocaust has to teach us."

This is a twelve-year-old. Okay? And I have like three hundred of these things. This is what I feel that I was spared to do. Teach these children. Now this child will never go through life with any hatred. She will respect other people. Her life has already changed.

Marty McMahon

Entrepreneur

My mother was one of my biggest inspirations. I wanted to make my parents proud. Trying to better myself. Creativity. Being able to see my creativity come to some conclusion inspired me. If I had an idea, I wanted to see it work. I wouldn't take no for an answer. I always felt that there was some way—a very positive outlook.

I think I've always been positive in my way of thinking. The one thing I have to say about that, though, is that when I do get an idea, I think very positively about creating something and then I will instinctively think of every negative reason as to what could go wrong with the situation. Then I weigh those factors and decide whether it's worth the risk, and then I either take it or I don't.

I want to mention my father here, too, because my father took the risk to come to this country and left everything that he had known in El Salvador. My father was from a privileged stock in El Salvador, and a crisis occurred in his life when his parents died and he absolutely lost everything. From someone who had been educated in England and never had to worry about earning a dime, he found himself with a young family, in a strange land. He took that risk because he also had the sense of adventure, which I also have. So I get the risk taking and the sense of adventure from my father and the creativity and imagination from my mother, and I think that's a really good combination for becoming an entrepreneur.

Jo Hanson
Artist/Environmentalist

I don't know whether I've got courage. I have a sense of necessity. I don't think I've ever felt courage. Possibly I've been involved in things that people would call courageous, but it seemed to me I was just doing what was necessary to do.

Mary Bitterman
President/CEO, public television

Motivation and courage —these are always very good questions. They're wonderful words, and they have a kind of lofty sense to them. And yet—I should think this is true of most people, and certainly of me—I didn't really stop and think about what motivated me. I think probably these are things that we only do after the fact, reflecting back.

What made me interested in working diligently, in learning new things, in preparing myself to make some contribution to the world in which I lived, probably was the example of people older than I was doing all kinds of jobs, doing them well, and really contributing to the progress of others. That to me seemed to be a pretty wonderful thing to do. Because I think my focus was always more external than internal. I was always trying to see what could be done to assist others, rather than just focusing on myself. There wasn't a lot of time to just sit around thinking about, "Am I happy? Am I unhappy today? How much do I expect from the world?" I'm part of the generation that remembers when John Kennedy said "It's not what your country can do for you, but what you can do for your country." That was the sort of attitude and set of values that I was brought up with.

And courage—I'm not sure that it was courage as much as a sense of stick-to-itiveness, of perseverance, and having the sense that any life lived should be as productive and constructive a life as possible. I've always thought that life was a very precious commodity and that one should never disparage the possibilities of what any single life can mean. And I think that commitment to the good life, in the sense of meaningful life, of contributory life, of ethical life, was very, very important to me. So it wasn't so much courage as a desire to proceed in a certain direction that I felt was constructive and would be a source of happiness for me, and would contribute to the progress of others.

Chapter 3

Overcoming Fear and Obstacles

I live with more fear and trembling than I had when I was younger. But it's kind of a delicious trembling, and I am now loyal to my fear . . . My life right now is one of mystery in honoring all that at one time I sought to leave behind me.

Sister Mary Neill

Many of us are consumed by fear. To a degree, our fear disables us from maximizing our potential. Similarly, all of us face obstacles on the path to fulfilling cherished hopes. How can we overcome or work through these times in our lives?

For many of the women in this chapter, these questions evoked recollections of profound moments when they were compelled to confront fear or respond to a seemingly impossible challenge. Their experiences illuminate how powerful our inner thoughts, attitudes, and imagination can be in helping to see us through times of terror, discouragement, and tragedy.

As I ponder their messages, I realize anew both the inevitability of risk and our freedom to choose our response to it. We become stronger not by seeking safety or avoiding difficulties, but by embracing our fear, seeking our individual sources of faith, and actively struggling with the challenges life places in our way.

Isabel Allende

Author

When people ask me, "What gives you the ability to bounce back?" my answer is very simple: I have no choice. There is no choice.

What could I do? My daughter was in a coma. She was recently married, practically on her honeymoon, when she had a porphyria crisis. Porphyria is a genetic condition she knew she had, so she took very good care of herself. Everything was perfect. She was very intelligent, and she had organized everything so perfectly that if anything happened to her she always had a strategy. Everything failed. This is karma. Everything failed. She was on vacation, she had an infection, she was menstruating. Everything combined together to produce a terrible crisis. She went to the hospital and they gave her the wrong drugs. The doctors created severe brain damage, but they didn't admit it. They didn't tell me. And so Paula remained in the hospital in intensive care for six months without the doctors admitting that she was never going to come out of the coma, because her brain was dead. And I stayed there with her until I was finally strong enough to pull her out of that place and bring her home, to the United States. Fortunately, her husband was very understanding, and he allowed me to do all this. He could have said, "No, she's my wife, and I'll take care of her." But he didn't. He allowed me to bring her back to my womb and my home.

People have often asked me, "How could you do all that? How could you take a person in a coma out of the hospital, place her on a United Airlines commercial flight, and bring her all the way, twenty hours flying, all the way to California to your house?" Well, I didn't have a choice. There was no choice. You cope with things as they come.

I went through the whole year one day at a time. One minute at a time I lived through her death . . . and maybe one year at a time I will get over it. But this is the way it happens, and you don't have much choice.

The great things that have happened in my life have often happened in spite of myself. Even the good things have happened without me planning them. I didn't plan to meet Willie on a book tour and fall madly in love and move into his house. How could I plan that? That's crazy. It just happened. Sometimes when I tell the story my friends say, "You were so brave! I would never move into a man's house and just invade his house!" I said, "Well, I was living in Venezuela. Either I would come to live with him, or I'd never see him again." So, you see, there were not many choices. Life puts you in a place where you have to do things. And I think that is what happened.

Lynn Woolsey

Congresswoman

I think the best and most meaningful story is when my children were one, three, and five years old and their dad—a manic-depressive and very successful businessman—totally lost it and wouldn't take charge of getting well or [taking his] medication, I left that situation with my children.

Here's a woman who was perfectly prepared to stay home and raise children for the rest of their lives, not even thinking what would happen in my own life. That's what I wanted to do. *Good Housekeeping* was my bible. I did have good job skills, and I had two years of college. I went to work with one-, three-, and five-year-old babies, and my pay didn't cover all of what we needed, so I started looking for a second job. I was going to be a waitress or something. A friend said, "Have you ever heard of Aid for Dependent Children?" I hadn't paid that much attention to it, but I went on welfare and kept working. Welfare paid for our healthcare and just enough extra money for childcare, and that kept things together for us for about three years while my career grew.

When my second son heard that about six years ago, he said, "We were never on welfare, Mother." I said, "We were. We certainly were. But that was the safety net we needed." I never looked at it as "What a bad person I am." I knew my kids needed it, it was there and we used it for what it was supposed to be—a safety net—and then we went forward and I became a much better person from the whole situation.

At thirty, with three young children, I had a rebirth. I moved from *Good Housekeeping* and being dressed to the nines all of the time and started a cystic fibrosis foundation in Marin County when my second child was brand new. It wasn't like I was just going to sit around and do nothing and not do meaningful things. My whole life changed, and I got to look at who Lynn Woolsey is, what my life was supposed to be.

Men would ask me out and say, "You have three children? Where do they live?" I'd be quite crude and say, "Where do you think they live, you son of a bitch? I'm their mother, they live with me. Hello and good-bye. Stay out of my life. What do you think you do? You have three children and you have a problem and you send them away some place? Where would they go?"

My mother was quite narcissistic, and never once when I was going through those hard times did I think about asking for help. Nor did I think about moving back home to Seattle. It wasn't that I disliked anybody. I loved my mother. But that was not what she was there for. I just had an internal knowledge that it was up to me. It got overwhelming sometimes, but I don't think I ever questioned that we'd be okay.

Carmel Greenwood
Entrepreneur

I think when I've been at the lowest ebb, some force comes in and I realize that I'm not alone. I have been down so low I've actually got down on my knees and asked for help, and help comes.

When I was writing my book, I felt full of energy and inspired. Then I decided that was my path—to just use my life as a personal example of hope. There is hope no matter how low you are, even if you're ostracized, as I was when I left my first husband. I had no friends, nothing. But then a divine force comes in that I believe is God, and you're not alone. And if you ask for help there's lots of your guides, your angels—whatever you'd like to call them—to come and help you.

Gretchen Dewitt

Public relations professional

My most challenging situation was the death of a child. That was something I could never have anticipated. I remember knowing women or men who had lost children, and I used to wonder how they could walk around. I thought, "If this ever happens to me, I couldn't survive it." Then it did happen to me, and I thought, "Well, I have to survive this because the options are really not great. It's self-destruction or survival."

And I wanted to do more than survive, I wanted to be happy. My first prayers were for strength, that I could keep walking and thinking and talking. As I grew stronger, I switched over to praying to find joy.

I had grown up really thinking that joy or happiness would be an inheritance that would be dropped in my lap, that it would be automatic. I would be given all good things because I was good, and nothing bad would ever happen to me because I was good and was therefore protected from bad.

And I learned that we're all, of course, at risk, and anything worth having is work. And happiness is worth having. So it's not just floating in the ocean without an effort. Everybody who's floating in the ocean is paddling like mad underneath the water to stay up. You don't just float. You have to work to stay up. So I worked at it.

I surrounded myself with things that would give me pleasure. I bought books that had beautiful pictures of flowers. I went to wonderful films. I remember the first one I saw after it happened was *A Room with a View,* and the music was beautiful, and the scenery was beautiful, and I knew I could feel joy again. It was hard work. Because all I wanted to do was be dead. So that was my most challenging situation. And I worked. I worked to be happy.

I maintained hope by talking to women who'd lost children, and I was reassured that one could not only survive, but be happy again. And because I have grown up in a Christian environment, I certainly believed in an afterlife. My hope was that life, whether it was a hundred years or six months, is brief on earth, but it's one room that we're in and then we go into another room. The hope—it's more than hope, it's a belief in an eternal nature of mankind, that the soul is not extinguished, that we live forever.

I used to play it back. I think everybody who has a tragedy, something terrible that happened, plays it back like it's a movie. Then you go back and say, "Okay, let's rewind this, and let's play it over and have it end up differently." And there was really no way. It wasn't that I had a son who'd fallen into a swimming pool when I wasn't watching. It was a crib death. He was six months old.

I thought of all the people who have children with heart defects, and who go to bed at night thinking, "Will he be awake in the morning, will he be alive?" I didn't have that worry before. It was just a terrible surprise.

We don't pick when people go. I don't think God's pulling strings or deciding who goes or when they go, or someone needs to be taught a lesson. I think we're here at risk. That was something that had nothing to do with God choosing that, or my not doing what I needed to do.

It just happened. No reason. But it changed my relationship, my feelings about God, because I had felt protected. And then I thought, "Well, why should I be protected? Nobody else is protected."

I can remember driving over to Oakland, and seeing druggies and their children running around on the streets, and thinking, "Those children are alive, and they've got parents that aren't really in great shape to take care of children, so why is mine dead?" I had a big feeling of abandonment. I felt abandoned by luck. By my baby. By God. I felt totally abandoned. I felt like a failure because I had not been able to keep a baby alive for me, for my husband, for my children who loved the baby.

I felt like a failure because I would have gone into a burning house and dragged him out, but I wasn't given the chance. I felt like a failure. So hope is that mortality is brief and we have to be a good sport about bad things that happen because the options, they're not good.

Leslie Young
Ballet soloist

It's trying to live each day without any regret, and that is a challenge in itself. Dancing—I could trip off the edge of the sidewalk and completely damage my career for the rest of my life. So ballet is something you can't take lightly. It can be taken away from you at any moment . . . So my challenge each day is to know that I feel completed and satisfied with what I've done in case I can't do it again the next day.

I guess one of the situations that made me clarify this so that it was more articulate was when I was rehearsing for a performance. It was five o'clock and the performance was at eight, and we had a rehearsal. It was a jump/slide, where you're supposed to slide on the edge of your toes across the floor with a partner who is supposed to help you. And our timing was off. So we did the jump and everything slid but my left foot. My foot sort of popped out of my shoe—the arch, the middle part of it—and you just know something is wrong. I had to sit down and I was out for the next six months, so I missed basically an entire season.

I remember sitting there icing and doing contrast baths where you're icing in one bucket of water, and you take your foot out and then you put it in hot water, and I thought, "This isn't happening!" I'd never been injured in my entire career. At one point I tried to put my pointe shoe back on, and I couldn't get my foot in my shoe, and I started to cry. I thought, "This could be it. I could be already done. I didn't get a chance to say good-bye to my career." But when I stopped to think about it, I really have worked every day, so that I don't feel that I am missing something. I've been doing that sort of naturally. But to actually have to vocalize that—to put a name on it—has affected me since then so that I could actually say, "I don't want to have any regrets with each day, each performance."

Granted, it's not going to be perfect every time, but that's not the point. If you have that effort in there, to really realize this could be it and this is your chance. It's your moment. We all have a gift to give, and I am the only one that can give my gift of myself, so this is my only shot at it.

Elizabeth Colton

Entrepreneur

Self-esteem is the key, because if you have the self-esteem, then you can overcome fear. So much of this is what this museum project is all about. It's about helping young girls and women develop self-esteem through inspiring stories and equal images from the past. If we learn about the past and see that only men played important roles, how are we going to be able to see ourselves as being able to play equal roles in the present or future? It's starting off with a loaded deck. So I think it is so critical that we celebrate not only the women who were the stars of history, if you will—the explorers, the inventors, the doctors—but also to celebrate the contributions that women in general made, to give value to women's thoughts and deeds in every way. Our traditional history doesn't do that.

Certainly I went through some low periods during my marriage where I was not recognized as a partner or as an equal, sometimes as even existing. I'm not sure what the process is through which one overcomes that. I know that now the thing that gives me courage to go out there every day, to walk into a room full of people I don't know at an event and start meeting people, is that I believe so strongly in this project. I am so certain that this project will be built and that it needs to be built and that it will be a wonderful addition to our cultural landscape and how we see ourselves as women and how men see us as women. I am so motivated by the worth of this project that I feel like I can do anything. So certainly that is one key, to believe in what you're doing.

Laurel Burch

Artist

I have faced very large challenges in my life and been able to, I guess the word is "overcome," but I don't want to fall into saying overcome. I think I would say that I innovated my way, or created my way, out of difficult challenges. I've always been able to do that.

Just having so many multiple fractures on top of each other, just over and over, having such escalation of my architectural fragility that there wasn't time to renew in between . . . For the first time I felt a loss of spirit when I'm really a very strong-spirited person. And what did I do about it? The way that I navigated my way out of that was through my memory of my ability to have done it before. So even though the circumstances were such that the mountains seemed higher and farther, I again used my imagination. I imagined that I could create an outcome that would be one of hope and life and passion again, even during times when I didn't feel that . . .

I was known for being such a bright and colorful and uplifted spirit. When I wasn't that way, I was very concerned not just about my view of myself, but about having that responsibility to be the caretaker of goodwill and an inspiration to others. That was really—that's my life's work. During that period where I didn't have that for myself, I couldn't provide it for others. And ultimately what happened is that for the first time in my life I really allowed myself to take care of my faith, and that was completely new.

There was a time when I wanted to take care of the world at large and everything in it, and even with my bones being what they were, I would dance on fractured legs and cut casts off and go to Egypt and drag my body outside the realm of what you could really do. But during the last several years, as I was maturing as a woman and coming into a different phase in my life, I got comfortable with my own healing and my own new picture of myself . . . The upside of that was having a front-row seat to the miracle that was trying to occur, actually watching and experiencing my bones healing over and over . . .

With this last round of multiple bones broken, there were times when I felt like I wasn't participating, that I was just so worn out. I felt, "I can't do this again, I just did this, and here it is again, and I have to start over." But just lying there in the hospital, I was seeing myself heal. I would see legs that were broken in half and then began to heal. So in a way it was just this miraculous thing. That's the upside of it, that you get this unbelievable sense of how precious everything is and how sacred.

My art has had, over these years, my ability to express this passion, and this preciousness of life really comes out. I chose a language to express that through images—that is my art.

Somebody asked me in the last few years if I ever painted my pain, and I said, "Why would I want to do that?"

Sue Backman

Entrepreneur/Billiards professional

I'm really not a fearful person. I believe fear is the great spirit killer, and I try to work through fear as quickly as possible when it comes up and look for the good side or the solution or the lesson or whatever. Basically for me it's like: "Okay. Something bad has happened. What's the lesson? What's the opportunity? What's the next step?"

So for me it's like a game. I don't always enjoy it at the time, but coming out of it successfully and coming to an acceptance or solution or whatever to get around it or to survive it—that's the good part.

Nancy Currie

Astronaut

The first thing I try to do is be as technically proficient as I can. I think back to when I first started learning how to fly, and I would look at these people who had been doing it for a long time and think, "Wow, how am I ever going to know all the details that they know about these systems?" But I guess my nature in anything I do is to dive into it. And I'm not an intelligent person. It is work. I'm not one of these folks that can look at something and automatically say, "Oh, I get it. I understand it." It's something I have to work at. But I'm almost driven to that. If I'm responsible for somebody else's life, I want to make sure that I've done everything within my capabilities to prevent anything from happening.

In terms of the fear, I guess the best analogy is getting ready for a shuttle launch, especially when you make that call to your family for the last time before you walk out to the vehicle, and you say good-bye. There's a certain amount of trust in God that you're going to be taken care of. And we do pray together; there are other Christian astronauts . . .

But I always tell people, when they ask "What are you thinking about when you get in a vehicle?" that I'm thinking about nothing but my job and the reactions I would have if something went wrong. So, the last thing I do is kneel down in prayer, and then when I get up and I walk in to get strapped into my seat, nothing goes through my mind except my task inside the shuttle. That's because you can go from being in an Apollo fire scenario, where you have to get out of the vehicle very quickly on the pad, to any variety of malfunctions that could occur during the ascent itself. And in my last flight's case, there was an awful lot of pressure on us because of the critical nature of the activities that we were doing to build the space station. There were thousands of folks waiting for us to do it correctly. So, literally, you don't think about anything other than your job and how best to do it.

Rabbi Stacy Friedman
Rabbi

I think my parents reared me to be very brave. Whenever I did big things or was going off to college or was doing other things, my mother would be, "Don't be afraid."

So I think for me, actually, my challenge in recent years has been opening up to fear and feeling fear. So it's really the opposite: living with fear and going forward nonetheless. In fact, I gave a sermon about this a couple of years ago at our high holidays because it was a big theme that I was working on in my life. I used this example: I was at Tassajara in the summer, and they had this cold plunge I was afraid to go into, and I didn't. And I said, "Before I leave, I'm going to walk right into this cold plunge." What did it for me was this little girl. She was ten or eleven years old, and I was watching how she did it. She was fearless, and I said: "How is it that you get into that water? I'm so afraid to get in because it's cold." She said, "I pretend I'm a fish and I just go in." I said, "Okay. I'm going to pretend I'm a fish." So I pretended I was a fish. I got in, and the water was freezing and it was really uncomfortable. But when I sat in it I realized that, number one, your body accommodates to it and you get used to it, and also that the cold wouldn't kill me and that it didn't matter if it was cold.

So I think part of it is just opening up to situations. I think about that little girl all the time: "I'm a fish." Or if I have to fly, "I'm a bird."

Another way I deal with fear is by putting myself in God's hands. I had a horrible flight incident where we were in a dangerous situation, and I turned myself over to God and also to the man next to me. He was grabbing me and holding me, and I got off the plane and ate two Snickers bars and thanked God for getting us there. But I put myself in God's hands, and that makes a difference.

Irene Zisblatt Zeigelstein
Holocaust survivor

After I was thrown out of school because I was a Jew, we went to school secretly, just for Jewish education. We used to go a couple of times a week and learn how to read and speak Hebrew. But that didn't last too long, because the curfews started and we couldn't go outside the house, and so that stopped. And of course they restricted us from everything else. They started taking away everything from us, so we were isolated, and that's when I was very unhappy. I couldn't understand this whole thing. From 1939 to 1944, things were just getting worse and worse . . .

Then we were taken to the ghetto. The ghetto was very congested with people from all over the region. We didn't have room in any of the buildings anymore, so my mother took the sheets and pillowcases out from the one suitcase we were allowed to take with us and built a sort of a hut. That was where we lived until the railroad was built and the trains with cattle cars came into the ghetto and then the deportation started.

The ghetto was also a holding place while they were building the railroad. And then they started to deport. They told us that we were going to a vineyard which was very famous in Hungary, and it made sense to us that we were going to a vineyard and work instead of being in this godforsaken place which had no food, no water, no sanitary facilities. We were guarded heavily by guards, and the men and boys were worked to death every single day. They would come home beaten, and some of them died, and so, of course, everybody had no problem getting on the cattle car.

But I had a problem because I didn't understand why we had to go in a cattle car, so I asked my father, "Why do we have to go into this train? What kind of a train is this?" He said, "Well, it is wartime, and they probably couldn't get the other trains over here. It's only a short ride, it will be okay." But when they loaded up the cattle cars and we were a hundred people in the cattle car with no light and when they closed the door and they bolted the door from the outside, I did not accept the fact that they didn't have any other train. I knew that something was very wrong, but I didn't know what. Nobody else did either.

The only light we had was a crack in the wall of the cattle car. After a couple of days, my father happened to be next to it and he looked back and said, "We're no longer going to the vineyard, because we just now crossed the border. We are out of our country and we are heading toward Poland." That shook everybody up, especially me, because I had heard a story when I was about ten years old from a man who spent the night in our house. He told my father to pack up his family and find a safe place to hide because the Germans in Poland were doing terrible things to the Jews. He told them a story about their taking Jewish infants and tearing them in half by their legs and throwing them in the Nostrum. I didn't know what the Nostrum was, but my father said, "A Nostrum is like a river. We have the Danube, and this is a river in the Ukraine called the Nostrum."

When my father announced that we were heading for Poland, I thought of that story. I was sitting on my suitcase, holding my little brother. He was two years old, and he was crying. He wanted to go home because he was hungry and cold, and I was assuring him that we would be home soon. But when I thought of that story, I hung on to him really tight and

I said to myself, "I will never let him go. They will never take him from me. They'll never do that to him." But they did other things to him . . .

And so I had a problem with that train, and I thought I was never going to see that door open. I was very, very nervous and upset, and the children were crying, and we couldn't help them, and it was just terrible. We went to the bathroom in that one pail and then when that filled up, we went to the bathroom wherever we stood because there was no room for moving around. The odor was terrible and people were getting sick, and they were crying and holding on to each other, and they were praying and screaming, and it was just an awful, awful five or six days, I don't remember.

When the doors opened and everybody thought that we were going to be given water and fresh air, what was awaiting us was not fresh water and not fresh air, but Nazi soldiers with dogs as big as I was and rifles and clubs, and they were yelling and the loudspeaker never stopped screaming. Orders were coming like every two seconds and while you tried to understand the first order, the second one was already there, and they were pushing and shoving and yelling, and it was just awful. I just could not grasp the, you know, the understanding of it, and I just wanted to die. But I couldn't die.

Jo Hanson

Artist/Environmentalist

I've thought about fear situations because I've certainly had my share of fear. There's only one occasion that I can recall where a dramatic event changed my fear.

In the 1960s I was preparing material for a major exhibition, the re-creation of a cemetery that was in southern Illinois. I had not known about it when I was growing up in that area. When I learned about it as an adult, I had about an acre or so of relatives in it.

I did rubbing the stones as a way of recording what was on them. When I spread them out, I saw that there was a language I didn't understand, and I don't mean a foreign language. I can tell you now that they reflect cultural change and attitudes. At that time I just knew they were saying things I didn't understand and that it would be meaningful for me to understand them.

I was flying back and forth periodically and doing work in that cemetery. To get into southern Illinois, the nearest city was St. Louis, and from there one would take a twelve-seater plane or smaller. I should say that I also grew up with an enormous fear of death that was well-founded in my experiences; I think there were things that had traumatized me and scared the wits out of me. So, on one of these trips in this little plane, suddenly an enormous electrical storm developed. Violent thunder and lightning flashed through the plane. The plane was tossing around like feathers on the wind. There was violent rain and wind, and there was no question that the plane would crash. The only question was how soon it would occur.

I was paralyzed by fear. So utterly paralyzed that I could not survive with it. I had to deal with it. I was so frozen by fear that I had to deal with it, and what came through my mind in a flash—a minute fraction of the time it takes to tell you about it—was a remembrance of two previous experiences.

One had been when I was a small child high in a cherry tree, where little girls are not supposed to be. I got so far out on the limb that the limb broke and I was really alarmed and figured I was going to get hurt. But this limb came down—the nicest ride you can imagine—and the landing was cushioned by the under-limbs and I had a ride that was better than any carnival you ever went to.

That flashed through my mind. That had been a very pleasant descent. Any descent would be pleasant like that, depending on one's attitude toward it.

The other thing that passed through my mind in the same instant was once when I'd been in a position to see something really beautiful and have an exciting experience and I'd been so afraid that I'd missed it all. What came into my mind was that the fall would not be unpleasant and that if I was so frozen with fear, I would already be dead and I wouldn't have these final minutes at my disposal when I could be enjoying them.

It sounds foolish. When I began to think this way, that I could enjoy the fall through the air and enjoy what I was seeing and the excitement of it, then I was able to see it, and it was one of the most beautiful, dramatic scenes I have ever seen.

I dove for my camera—I was into aerial photographs at the time. By the time I got my camera out of the case, the storm broke and all of this settled down and I didn't get any pictures, but I also didn't die.

I've never since then been afraid on a plane again. I simply got the cure.

What I discovered in my work with this cemetery was the other process—a more evolutionary process. As I worked on that project, I felt I was dealing with cultural change and cultural understanding and my own roots. It took me about two years after the exhibition started showing to realize that other people were reacting to it as a discussion of death and the natural processes of death. They were not paying attention to my cultural history at all.

After about two years, I began to realize that yes, I was talking about death, and I did find that my own fear had dissipated in the process of working with the issue even though I didn't know I was working with it.

I think there's this thing we call aesthetic distance, when you're working with something and it's emotionally strong, as our work often is. At the same time that you're dealing with the strong emotion, you're dealing with the aesthetic decisions of how to make a presentation that other people will find meaningful. I think that when you work with things and what is called an aesthetic distance, it allows you to approach and discuss in your mind issues that might be too difficult if you went at them directly.

Through that process I lost my fear of death altogether. I just don't have it anymore.

Those are two ways of dealing with fear, and I suppose there are a lot of other ways. Mainly those are the ways that I call necessity. You have to do something, so you do it.

Mary Bitterman
President/CEO, public television

I don't want to make it sound as though I'm not a reflective person, but I must say that for various reasons, and because of various circumstances, I have moved fairly quickly through life. What do I mean by that? There weren't large portions of my life in which I would sit down and say, "Am I afraid to do this?" Because from the time that I was very small, I had serious responsibilities at home. I worked from the time I was twelve. I always had things that needed to be done and tried to prepare myself as well as I could for any of those things that I needed to do, whether it was preparing for an examination, or traveling to the East Coast to go to university for the first time in my life—to go to a completely strange place where I had never been before, to Georgetown University, to the School of Foreign Service. And at that time there were just a handful of women. It was an all-male environment. Getting off the plane and finding my way to Georgetown, and finding my way through everything, I really didn't have a lot of time to think about overcoming any fearful sense of the situation, but just keeping my wits and doing what had to be done.

I've always been very hopeful, and I think that it's been a kind of guiding mechanism for me. I think of Goethe's statement that there is nothing so characteristic of man as his ability to live on hope. I've always remained very hopeful that with proper communication, with doing your job right, with respecting others and the rest of it, you can every day do better tomorrow what you did today. And by doing that I think the maintenance of the appropriate level of self-esteem is kept.

Sister Mary Neill
Nun/Author/Educator

One of the things I'll say about being a nun is, again a quotation, "You are as strong as whatever you struggle with." To be a nun is to struggle with these structures, these religious structures, and then there is the struggle with God. And so I have become strong. But it is a strange kind of strength. At a workshop once some woman stood up and said her little poem, and she said, "I have grown strong through much trembling." I would say about this strength that I have, I've grown strong through fighting. I've been scarred by that, I've been the warrior woman. And I've been growing strong through trembling. Religiously speaking, that is what the definition of the Holy is—that which is fascinating and also fear making.

So at sixty-six, I live with more fear and trembling than I had when I was younger. But it's kind of a delicious trembling, and I am now loyal to my fear . . . My life right now is one of mystery in honoring all that at one time I sought to leave behind me—befriending really profoundly all of me that was weak or pathological or weird or crazy.

Jeanne Rizzo
Entrepreneur

I had absolutely no experience. I was trained as a nurse. I had to learn things. I had to learn about accounting, I had to learn about the business. I had to learn about music. It never occurred to me that I couldn't. It never occurred to me that those weren't just things to learn.

I knew how to build a team, how to work with people to have them be part of the family and take pride. I always understood that if everyone working there felt pride in what they were doing, we would have a better product.

I had to overcome being a woman in the business. I actually had musical performers who refused to take their pay from me because I was a woman, male performers who didn't want me to tell them to go onstage or didn't want to take my phone calls when I would call to book them. I was absolutely astounded by that—that being a woman in the music industry was not readily accepted—and I had to overcome that. So that was a challenge for me, to find ways to do that and convince people that I was credible.

I think that after being furious for a period of time and trying to be insistent and what not, I tried to demonstrate that what we were doing was really important and it was credible work and I would get references from people to other people. So I spent a lot of time calling booking agents on the phone and talking with them—spending more time than I think my male counterparts had to do—and turning out a good product over and over and keeping all the reviews and sending them out to people so that people could see that what we were doing was valuable. So I just had to communicate a lot more. I had to convince more people where maybe a male promoter wouldn't have to send a deposit on an act where we did because we were new and they were talking to a woman on the phone. We had to do that and convince people that we were credible.

So it took a while, but ultimately the reputation of the Music Hall stands on its own, and I feel proud to have accomplished that. But it wasn't easy. That was a challenge for me. Being in a business during the eighties when drugs were so rampant was also difficult for me. Dealing with musicians when there was a lot of drugs and alcohol around and being in the bar business and trying to reconcile that—that was a personal challenge for me.

Chapter 4

Passion for Your Destiny

I once heard someone say something very important that I keep in mind. "Whatever you do, you offer." It's an offering. How that offering is going to be received by the forces of nature, by the gods, by people, we don't know. It's none of my business. My business is to present this offering in a lovely way.

Isabel Allende

The women in this book represent all walks of life. I wanted to know, what brought them to their passion, their life's work? Did they have a sense of destiny?

Many of these women feel that following your passion *is* your destiny. Finding out what you love to do, and having the ambition to follow that path, brings fulfillment and happiness into one's life. And if you have the courage to do what you love, you are more capable of enjoying the journey, not just the outcome.

As a young man, Vincent van Gogh once said that his mission was to teach people to "love what you love." Van Gogh said that although it sounds easy, it is very hard to do.

Another common thread in the responses of most of these women was that following one's passion or destiny inevitably involves others besides oneself. It is not just a matter of finding what makes each of us happy; it is also a matter of contributing our individual strengths and talents for the common good.

Isabel Allende
Author

Have I ever had a sense of destiny? Yes. When I was young I always had the feeling that I could do much more, that I had potential and I had not found my niche. I had not found what I was good for. I suspected it had to do with writing because all my life I had written. Journals. Journalism. Letters. A letter every day for thirty-five years to my mother. So I had always been on the periphery of literature, never daring to say "I want to write, I want to be a writer," because it sounded so pretentious. Women were not supposed to be creative in my generation in Chile. It would have been very pretentious, laughable, to say I wanted to make a living writing novels.

Creativity was never encouraged for a woman in my house or in that generation, or in the country where I lived. I was supposed to work, to help my husband through the first years, and that was it. And always support him so that he would be the provider, because his life was much more important than mine. Now that I look back, I realize that I was much more intelligent than he was. He was intelligent—probably in a more scientific way—but I was street-smart, which he wasn't. He always lived in theories, in ideas, and could never deal with life. I was always in the street as a journalist, vibrating with whatever was happening in the world. Raising children, taking care of a family. For many reasons, my life was just as important as his, but I didn't know that then. It took me many, many years to learn that. After I divorced him, I realized that I was smarter, that I had better chances than he did to make another life. And that is exactly what has happened.

I always felt, before I started writing, that I hadn't found what I wanted to do, that I was wasting my time. By the time I was forty, I hadn't done anything that was memorable or significant or transcendent, and I felt very frustrated. I would often say: "Well, maybe I'm not anything special. Maybe I'm just like everybody else, and that's why I haven't done anything special." That is what I was asking myself all the time when I started to write. When I started writing, I didn't know that I was writing a book. I didn't know what lay ahead of me. I didn't know that the book was ever going to be published or if it was going to be successful. So things simply happened, one at a time . . . I just put a lot of work into everything, and I don't think of the outcome. I think of the process. I love the process of what I do. So if it's successful or not, well, it doesn't matter.

I once heard someone say something very important that I keep in mind: "Whatever you do, you offer." It's an offering. How that offering is going to be received by the forces of nature, by the gods, by people, we don't know. It's none of my business. My business is to present this offering in a lovely way.

When I went to Bali, I saw that women wove little baskets, four baskets a day, all different, to present little offerings of flowers and seeds and incense to the deities they have in their home. There are usually more than six deities in each house, and each one needs an offering four times a day. Multiply and see how many baskets they weave, automatically, while they do other things. And each one is lovely, so their offering is lovely. You make it lovely with work and effort. Now, how it's going to be received, we don't know. I can't know that, so I don't worry.

I am in touch with what I want to write. What I feel. Every book echoes something that I am at that moment, or something that has happened to me. Now if that coincides with what the world wants or the publisher wants, perfect. But often it doesn't, and it doesn't matter. I will not betray myself in order to write something that is commercial—something that people want to receive, or a sequel of what was successful before. Each book is new; it's an experiment. I have to invent everything again and again. I haven't learned much. But I can't betray that force inside me, because if I do I will break the magic. It would be like using the magic for something bad, and I'm very superstitious. I think it will turn against me like a boomerang! I'm very careful with what I say, what I do, the way I love, because I'm superstitious. I always see the consequences of things.

Cause and effect. We live so fast that we think we can just do anything—scattering dirt and garbage all over the place, thinking we won't suffer the consequences. But we do; we always do. Everything comes back. It's just amazing. The good and the bad always come back.

Gretchen Dewitt
Public relations professional

My destiny was to be a mother. A good one, but not a perfect one. I was surprised at how imperfect I was as a mother. But I wanted to be a mother. I have always wanted to have children. That was what I wanted the most out of my life. And I've gotten it.

I've had this repetitive dream. Repetitive dreams are the dreams you listen to because it's your psyche giving you a message, knocking on your door. My repetitive dream is that I've been in a house. I'm getting ready to leave the house because it's too small. Then I discover rooms that have been there all the time, and I didn't know they were there. I didn't go into the rooms. Of course, the house is the persona, and these are the different areas that I need to explore.

And so my destiny was to be happy. I wanted to be happy. I wanted to be good. I wanted to be a mother. And I wanted to maximize whatever potentials I have. So if it was going to be in athletics, or in music, or in writing, I wanted to maximize what I thought I could do. I wanted to do it as well as I could do.

Alice Waters
Restaurateur/Author/Educator

There is an idea that came from my work at the restaurant. I felt like we were all interconnected, and there wasn't a possibility for me to have a restaurant on a little island and expect that we could provide all our own food and not be contaminated in any way by what's upstream. So I imagined that we needed to reach every kid in this country, and the best way to do that is through the public school system. I imagined sort of an ecological curriculum that could teach children certain values, essential values I call them, that help them live in the world and find meaning in their lives. So the idea is to give them time to work in a garden, to cook in the kitchen, and time to sit at the table. I think that that whole experience can be transformational, really transformational. I've seen kids' lives change through that experience.

So I could imagine this to be a national curriculum. I was doing a pilot project at this middle school. Ultimately I would like to see it in every school in this country, and every school in the world. Kids should learn how to take care of the land, be good stewards, learn how to cook for themselves, so that they ultimately can cook for their family and their friends. And sit around the table, because that's where communication happens. It's a very important ritual. That's definitely a core belief that I have, that making the right choices about food can bring you not only pleasure in nourishment but it can bring the sense of family and the sense of community.

That I think kids are particularly hungry for. Everybody's hungry for that. They just don't know it.

That's the breakdown of our culture, when we don't sit around the table. It's changing. It's changing in France. It's changing everywhere. As soon as they find an easier way to do it, they want to do that. I don't think people know what they're sacrificing.

Well, we're doing it. We got one thousand kids there, and they're going to build a cafeteria in the next two years, and we've got already a kitchen classroom, and a garden classroom, and we'll see what happens.

Madeleine Albright
Former Secretary of State

On a personal level, I enjoy every day. Foreign policy in this era is an endlessly fascinating and terrifically fast-paced operation. This is fortunate, because there's something to be said for not slowing down.

Shortly before Christmas, I took a few days off. That first morning, I sat down, put my feet up and had a nice leisurely read of the newspapers. This was a big mistake—no wonder so many people are depressed! It is inherent in the job of Secretary of State and, I think, partly inherent simply in being an American, that you begin to feel responsible even for events you cannot control. It is particularly frustrating to me when areas or problems that seem to be going in the right direction stall or slip backward.

Like most Americans, I am goal-oriented, and I wanted to start a task and finish it and move on to the next one. But diplomacy today does not lend itself to that. Instead, it's like trying to fold one of those cardboard boxes. You get the corners in place, but they all start to come undone when you try to fold the fourth one. The danger is that we will grow frustrated and simply walk away from the hard problems in strategic regions such as the Balkans and the Gulf, or that we will become impatient and act rashly without sufficient preparation or careful weighing of the risks. If we are to protect our nation's interests, we must be persistent in our policies, realistic in our expectations, true to our principles, and firm in our actions.

I don't think everything I do every day is perfect, but I really am having a wonderful time—knock on wood!

Leslie Young

Ballet soloist

I wasn't one of those little girls with the dream of being a ballerina one day. I just knew that I loved to dance.

Even though you're always working for a performance, you still don't lose sight of the future, of what you're working toward. But it is important to enjoy each little step along the way, the process, and still be able to have your sight up ahead, on your goal.

If you're walking on a path, you're enjoying the flowers and the birds singing and the sunshine on your face, you're enjoying exactly where you are. But you can also see ahead of you. You can also see behind you. You're just trying to enjoy the whole picture, but still realizing where you are at that moment.

I think you're surrounded by people that have a different timing in their life. There are people who race ahead of you, even though you started in the same place. And sometimes it's hard. But I'm not them. That's their destiny, I guess, in life. And that's their pace. But this is mine, and I need to learn to appreciate my own life and not wish for someone else's because they seem to be going there faster, with more glory. I know it's not about that.

Annelies Atchley

Artist/Educator

I wanted to be a ceramist. When I was sixteen, I could take a hunk of clay and make your face—totally, exactly you. My mother wanted me to go to the sculptress who did Gandhi and all the famous people of the world. She wanted me as an apprentice. That's when my fight with my mother started. I said, "I want to mold real flesh. I don't want cold clay." So that's how I became a kindergarten teacher.

My mother never forgave me that I wasn't going on my talent. My talent was to do sculpting. I'd just take a hunk of clay and ten minutes later you were in that clay. I could feel the depth and everything and just do it. I don't know where it comes from. It just comes from within. I look at you and I do it on the clay, and it is there.

I did that when I was sixteen when I was given as an au pair to a family. I did his bust and her bust, and that family really appreciated me. They thought I was very talented. I sewed with the kids and did a lot of incredible things with the children.

From there I went to university and skipped two years of school. So then I had to have a profession, and I became a kindergarten teacher. Edith Markson knew that I did puppetry and made dolls and did all these sculpture things with the kids. I said, "I want to be a ceramist." She said, "Go to Italy. That's where you belong."

I left the United States to earn a little more money in Switzerland and then go to Italy. Then my mother said, "You can't stay here. Not even three weeks." So I immediately found a place in Italy through some people and enrolled in a famous ceramic school in Firenza.

Laurel Burch

Artist

The word "destiny" is almost like a destination, an ultimate destination. It's a word that I like, but I think of it as changing. It evolves.

It's a hard thing to talk about with words anyway. It's something that I have sense of, but it's hard to find words to put around it. I think my life has certainly been influenced by having a free spirit and a creative spirit, and a fragile body. Those things are really kind of contradictory in a way, because it's having boundaries and being boundless at the same time—boundary-less. And so I think a lot of my destiny, a lot of my journey, has to do with those two things, the experience of being completely earthbound and inside of a body that has unusual circumstances and then having a spirit that's just completely transcendent . . .

In terms of having a direction or a strategy or path, it has really changed dramatically depending on the circumstances. My evolution is impacted so strongly sometimes. I guess that's true with everybody, but I think in a lot of ways my creative spirit has been able to develop and express itself out of finding ways to understand my circumstances. A specific example would be that from the time that I was really small, a lot of my well-being and my sense of who I am and what I'm passionate to do has to do with connectedness with others in a very spirit-oriented place. If something happens where I am not able to connect in those ways or make something, or innovate something for people because of the circumstances, then I have found other ways to do that. So, if my hands are broken, I can't make something and offer it to someone. But I found that I could create through the way that I said what I said, or express myself. Sometimes I would sing, sometimes I would dance. Sometimes, if I couldn't dance, or move, or walk, I would paint, or write little stories, or do all different kinds of innovative things. They all had to do with a feeling that always wants to create and express and offer. A lot of inner strength has come out of that challenge.

I think I would say that passion and courage are the two things that I have more of than anything. People use the word "talent." I don't identify with that word at all. But courage and passion came out of an absolutely insatiable love of life and appreciation for it, out of understanding at a very early age the preciousness of it, how quickly something could happen and change. The way it manifested for me was in having a greater passion for life and appreciating every second, savoring every little tiny moment . . .

Courage has always been something that evolved out of the passion. For me it follows passion. I have an insatiable passion to do something, or to give something. That is where the courage comes from to stand up on my leg for the first time after it's broken, because I want to get somewhere. There's always some new magical, wonderful place that I want to go and to experience and show people. A lot of times it takes courage to do that.

I think the state of courage is something that I have. I think of it as a natural thing. I had to conjure it up a lot of times, remember that I had it, but for the most part, it is a kind of natural state.

Nancy Currie
Astronaut

I always compared being in this job to my Mount Everest. Or my marathon. Or whatever it is that people say, "Gee, someday I'd really like to go do that." That was this job for me: "Some day I'd give anything to come do this job."

I always tried to enhance my qualifications and better myself to make myself a little more competitive. But never for one minute did I think I would actually be selected. There was no one more surprised than I was when I was selected.

Rabbi Stacy Friedman
Rabbi

There's a Jewish expression that says everything is foreseen, but free will is given. Sometimes people say, "Do you believe in fate or destiny?" I believe that there is a destiny or master plan that God has in store for us or that we are a part of by being people of this universe. But within that, we also have free will. Just because something might be established in the cosmos for me doesn't mean I have to sit here and wait for something specific to happen. Part of that destiny is in my control. Part of it is through my intellect and emotions and spirit and body and my interaction with you, and all these sorts of things.

I really believe that there is a greater plan. There's a greater universe operating. We're not in as great control as we think we are. I think we're in control within certain limits and that trying to tap into what that larger plan is or what that other world is that's going on simultaneously is a really important thing to do. For me, that's what the Sabbath is about. In the Jewish tradition, on the seventh day we're supposed to mimic God's resting from creation. So we don't create on the seventh day, which traditionally means that we don't build or use money or cook with fire, do errands, do the laundry. We live in a world that is an "as if" world. We live as if everything were perfect. When we do that, we stop trying to control things and become part of it. You know when you're right on top of the wave and you feel the wave as opposed to fighting everything and trying to control things? I think that's when we get in touch with our destiny.

Reverend Veronica Goines
Presbyterian pastor

I went through a period of time where I felt this tugging because it felt like I was living two parallel lives. There was all of this interconnection, but at the same time I was more drawn in the area of my faith and my religious life and that aspect of my life that had to do with caring and administering to people. I loved the graphics field and I loved the work that I did and the illustrations that I could produce and the challenge that it was mentally, but it was really beginning to wane in comparison. So as I was struggling to try to come to terms with this, I remember sitting on the top side of my bed near the pillow, as I was sitting there I really started talking to God. I was saying, "Okay, God. If this is something that you want me to do, then I will surrender but I just need to know if this is truly what you want me to do." It began this dialogue between us that with each moment became more clarifying. There were scriptures that came to me that I certainly had no remembrance of ever putting to memory. These weren't verses that were very familiar to me, but they came to me at that time. They basically confirmed that it was like God saying, "It's no mistake that I'm calling you. This isn't something that I'm doing as an afterthought. Before the worlds were even formed I knew that this would be your calling." It was incredible because it was so clear and convincing.

Just being there in the midst of this prayer time, there were other things that the Lord dealt with. I remember thinking and feeling "I just feel so unworthy." A lot of that was thinking, "Here I am, a divorced person, and how am I going to do ministry?" Then I heard the Spirit whisper to me, "Don't think I'm surprised by anything that has happened in your life. Nothing in your life has taken me by surprise. The gifts of calling that I have given you are irrevocable. I won't take them back no matter what has happened in your life."

So it was just this incredible time in which not only did I come to this place of complete peace, but as I sat there at the head of my bed with my arms extended to the ceiling and as I was praying, I just felt this incredible weight lift off of me. All of the doubts and fears I had about doing ministry dissipated. What was left in their place was this incredible joy and this feeling of complete fullness. It was almost as though I was just buoyed and held up by this joy as though I weren't really sitting on the bed at all. I was just kind of floating in midair. It was really profound.

A part of what happened during that time was hearing these scriptures and a part of it was the connections to my past. At that moment was when I remembered the thoughts I had as a child at five years old, when I was watching this missionary film at our church and something was just tugging on my heart. It was a film on folks in Africa and some were suffering, and so forth. It was like this thing about ministry, but I didn't have words for any of that. So I wouldn't have been able to articulate it, but I just saw these people who were hurting. Then again I remembered in the eighth grade having an experience of this clarity, and I somehow knew that I was going to go into the ministry. I remembered telling my boyfriend, and he looked at me and said, "You mean you're going to become a nun?" I said, "No, I don't think so." It was like I knew God had something for me, but I again didn't know what to call it because in the eighth grade I didn't even know a woman minister. Later, when I got ready to go away to college, immediately I was looking for some type of theology or biblical studies, and I didn't necessarily know why.

So I could just see a lot of places in my life where something would emerge and then recede. When it was time, it all came together.

Irene Zisblatt Zeigelstein

Holocaust survivor

Once I reached out to hug my mother, and of course she wasn't there. So I sat down on the floor and I wrote her a letter. She asked me to do something and I couldn't answer her; she was gone. So this is what I wrote to her: "I will not cry anymore, and I will never forget the lives of the children who died a cruel death because they were Jewish. I will never forget the painful look in their eyes when they marched to their deaths. Dear Mother, this letter I am writing to you is very special. I want to tell you how much I missed you. I missed you on my wedding day; you did not share in my happiness. I missed you when I gave birth to your grandchildren and you could not hold them. It is difficult to live with the fact that you were cheated of enjoying that. As for me, being a mother today, I can feel the pain you felt when your children died in your arms from the gas. For me there is no medicine I can take to heal the pain. I am still learning to live with it. I promise to tell the world all that happened and I hope that God will help me stay strong, and I pray that he watches over our children of tomorrow so they can remember the past and never be silent when they see injustice against people. What happened to us should never happen again."

So I made a commitment to help heal the sense of hatred, and when I can't help heal anymore, I hope to sit in my chair and tell them that they are being remembered because we are telling what they want us to tell.

People wanted to hear my story. I had no problem telling all. I couldn't remember at that time as much as I remembered after. But whatever I remembered just came out of me with no problem. I felt that this is my commitment and this is my duty. This is what I have to do and as long as I am strong enough to do it, I made a commitment to do it, and that's probably the reason that I was spared.

People call me to speak. I don't do this for money. I don't do this for fame or anything. I do it so I can teach the children. I can't teach them to understand the Holocaust because there is no understanding. There is not any possible way that anybody can understand the Holocaust. But they can have an understanding of the teaching from the Holocaust. Because the Holocaust teaches us what can happen to people because of apathy. That's what I am trying to teach, tolerance and to heal the hatred and to build a better future for our children and grandchildren and great-grandchildren.

Marti McMahon

Entrepreneur

My dream was to create the best charter company on San Francisco Bay with vessels that would be homey and yachty-looking and noncommercial, offering a personal service to many, many clients, and one day to eventually build a boat from scratch. I had, at this point in my life, renovated many, many boats, and they were all pretty bad when I acquired them. My creativity and imagination that I got from watching my mother gave me the know-how to make these boats turn into something quite lovely with very little money. So each boat that was renovated and sold became a profit center to give me more money to get a larger boat that also needed some tender, loving care, and then I turned that boat around and made a profit on it.

So my dream was to build a boat one day from scratch, one that I could design the way that I thought the ideal charter yacht should be. Eventually I was able to do that, but I was turned down by many, many banks when I tried to get the money to do that. So it wasn't a matter of doing it within a year or two. It was a matter of probably a five- or six-year venture.

I think that I always felt that I wanted to be able to make a mark in some way, somehow to touch people's lives. I didn't know how that was going to happen, but I've always been a very happy person. I love people, absolutely love people, and I have a genuine warmth for meeting them and making them feel at home. So with my business I have been able to touch many, many people from all over the world. I feel pretty blessed that I have created a business on beautiful San Francisco Bay, one of the most beautiful bays in the world, and that I can touch these people, not only people that come on board to take a cruise with us and taste our wonderful food, but also many people who have worked for me along the way. Some of them have gone on to become entrepreneurs themselves.

I think entrepreneurs have to have a tremendous amount of energy, but they also have to have a lot of answers to questions that come up, to find solutions and just never say no. I mean they just will not be stopped. I guess that's what distinguishes a successful entrepreneur—someone who doesn't relent and say, "It's not going to work."

Jo Hanson

Artist/Environmentalist

I've never had a sense of destiny. Recently I was reading something about Mesopotamian mythology, and it suggested that destiny and fate were two different things in mythology. Destiny is what is unchangeable, and fate is what you can work with.

I actually have no sense of either one. My experience is that one thing leads to another leads to another. I guess I have an avid interest in where things lead, so I keep going.

Mary Bitterman
President/CEO, public television

I was brought up in a household where both of my parents were public servants. My mother was a teacher in the public schools, and my father was a judge. They were the first generation in their families that was able to go to university and fulfill part of the American dream. They were very conscious of the responsibility they had because they had had that opportunity, my mother to go to San Jose State, which was then San Jose Normal School, a teachers' school, and my father to Santa Clara University on a scholarship.

I think the way my parents brought me up, it wasn't the notion of some highfalutin' destiny—that you will be this or that or whatever. It was more the idea that you have an opportunity. Because you enjoy good health and because you are able to get a good education, you have the opportunity to become a person of some substance. You can make some material contribution to the society in which you live, and there's nothing more precious or noble than that. So, don't let this opportunity go. And so it was that sense that if you start off life with good health and with the opportunity for education, then there is concomitant responsibility.

Sister Mary Neill
Nun/Author/Educator

I did my doctoral dissertation on the religious thought of John McMurray. He was living at the time; he was in his eighties. He's a famous British philosopher. He's not well known in the United States, but he's very popular in England. He said that other hands brought us from the womb, and other hands would place us in the tomb. We are always delivered by others' hands. I think with women, who are raised to be dependent or codependent, we have to move out of that kind of giving of self that comes from the cultural roles and from our own masochism. We have to become strong and warriorlike and then in order to be women, we have to practice radical dependency.

I see that in Christ, like he's in agony. He says, "Pray with me, stay with me. Do you love me? Do you love me?" Very often Christ is portrayed as this really independent figure, but I think what he exemplifies is radical dependence . . .

When I was young, I had this hunger for God. It's very strange, a very weird call. It's to say, "God, I give you everything." I really meant it—"I give you my whole life, everything." And to see if God said to me, "Thanks, but you're not that interesting. Get a self!"

So I have gotten a self. I've traveled abroad. I've done books. I've got distinguished. Now I have a self. And I'm not that interested in giving it up to God. But now it's the time, because it takes a really strong self to give up a self. Most people give it up so they can move through someone else's self. No, that's not it. You give it up so that it's given back to you.

So I would say that spiritually where I am now, the prayer that I say over and over is to be called to greater and greater liberty, greater and greater freedom. Freedom to be afraid, to feel the darkness and the incompletion and the chaos.

My favorite book about Jesus is *Jesus Means Freedom*. It's a very scary thing to be called to. So the prayer that I say over and over is, "Lord, receive my liberty, my understanding, my will. You have given all to me, I give it back to you. Give me your grace and your love. That's enough for me."

Jeanne Rizzo
Entrepreneur

When I got involved with the man I wound up marrying, we had a love of music together, and we would go to New York and listen to music all of the time. We were both interested in leaving the New York area, and we moved to California. We moved to San Francisco, and we realized that the music scene—the jazz music scene—was not flourishing the way it was in New York. So we said, "Wouldn't it be great to have a little jazz piano bar?"

Suddenly I had to realize that my destiny was not based on my profession but on following something that I had a passion for. I have this passion for music. When I took the Florence Nightingale pledge as a student nurse back in the sixties, I vowed to be the handmaid of the physician. I realized, "I don't want to do that. I don't want to be the handmaid of the physician." I wanted to decide: "Am I a nurse because I thought those were my only options?" It's not that I didn't love it. I worked at Marin General as the head nurse and had a good job. All that was fine. I excelled in it, but I didn't feel a passion for it.

At the point when Tom and Sam Duvall and I decided that we wanted to open up some kind of a music club in San Francisco, I found I had great passion for that, for the idea of creating something that didn't exist and being part of a team that would do that. So we opened up the Great American Music Hall, and at that moment I understood that I didn't know what my destiny was, my definition of destiny being the work that I would do. I had to come to understand it in some other way. It wasn't that I wasn't any longer a nurse or a nightclub owner. My destiny was going to be determined by following my passion and following things I felt I could make a difference in. I loved bringing good and great music that people wanted to hear and creating the events and being in the audience. I absolutely loved that, and I also knew that I had a responsibility to use that forum to make a difference in terms of my political activism. So once a month at least I would have some kind of a benefit concert, whether it was Project Open Hand or Bread and Roses or the Lyon Martin Clinic, and I loved that. I had this opportunity—this platform—to bring social issues and entertainment together and use this place that I had to make a difference. That kept me motivated through the hard music times, when we went from booking only what we wanted to hear to booking things that we had to book in order to make money.

So I think that determining my destiny was a matter of knowing that I had to feel passion and commitment to it, and it had to make a difference. I really felt that my job was to make a difference in the world, that I had something to bring and that I could leave the world a better place. It never occurred to me that I couldn't.

Chapter 5

The People in Your Life

> You must always be mindful of the gratitude that is appropriate to extend to all of those people, whether teachers, or family, friends, or relatives, or people you met at different points in your life, who had some confidence in you, who gave you a chance. That's what makes a difference.
>
> *Mary Bitterman*

We have all heard John Donne's words "No man is an island." For the women I spoke with, Donne's words are much more than a proverb; they are a lived reality. These women experience a web of interconnection, not only with family, friends, and professional colleagues, but with women and men of history who inspired them by their example.

Other people can help us follow our paths in so many ways, whether by inspiring us, supporting us in some way, becoming mentors, or simply offering their love. To listen to the women in this chapter is to know that we are social beings who need others to help us create the lives we live.

Isabel Allende

Author

Who helped me? Oh, everybody helped me. My mother, first of all, by loving me unconditionally. Before I was born, she loved me. I hadn't been born for five minutes and she was already willing to give her life for me. This is unconditional love. With this platform, I can walk, I can fly, I can swim, I can do anything if I have this sort of emotional platform on which to stand.

They say that you need just one person to love you unconditionally, to be able to grow healthy, and I think she was it, and that's wonderful. My mother was enough.

I've always had a man in my life who has loved me, which I'm very grateful for. Not because I think that I couldn't live without a man, but because I'm a very sexual person, and sex has been important in my life. The fact that I have never had to compromise to get it is good! It's good, because I know I would compromise. I hope that my hormones will finally release, and some day I will be able to live without being, not determined, but motivated so strongly by sexuality. I'm looking forward to that. It will be a moment of great freedom! I know that many of my friends have reached that wonderful, sublime, and spiritual state in which they don't need a man. Oh, my God, I'm looking forward to that, but I'm not there!

I have my stepfather now who has been a best friend, not so much a father as a great friend. I have two children with whom I have such clear communication, and I still have it with my daughter, although in a different way. I know that whatever happens my son Nicholas will be there, like my mother, and he'll take care of me. And I know that in another dimension, in a spiritual dimension, Paula takes care of me. It's not that I believe that her ghost will be like an angel flapping wings behind me. No. But her memory is so strong that I can always go back to her, and I do several times a day. In many moments I just go inside, and she's there. I once said in a speech that it was as if I had a little chair inside and she would be sitting on that chair, rocking in that chair permanently. One week later I received in the mail a little chair that a person sent me. I've kept it to remind me that this is a wonderful metaphor of how I see my daughter, just sitting there calmly. The memory is there, and I can always look back at the twenty-seven wonderful years that we shared and be grateful for them. I try to remember moments in which I needed her advice or companionship, and what she did at that time. Then, when I need that same thing today, I can always reach into that storage place in my memory and get what I need from her, or from my grandfather, or from my mother-in-law. Or even from my mother, who is alive but lives in Chile. Perhaps I can't bother her at a certain time with something that might hurt her, so then I look at the letters in my closet. I have packages with the letters that she has written to me every single day of her life, and I can always look for a letter that will help me. It's like those people who open the Bible at any page and they find an answer. I can do the same with my mother's letters. So all that has helped.

Carmel Greenwood

Entrepreneur

Who helped me? Well, I must say that when I asked for help, I met my future husband, John, who helped me to regain my dignity.

My older children in that time helped me tremendously. I remember one time when my daughter stood up at school, she was twelve, and they were asking, "What does your mother do?" My daughter said, "She's a stockbroker. She flies airplanes, she parachutes, and she's a national scuba diver instructor." The other children said she was lying. She looked astonished and said, "Well, don't all mothers do that sort of thing?" [Laughter]

I remember with my ex-husband, when I got up at four o'clock in the morning and put on my big boots to make a parachute jump, he said, "I knew you're mad. Now I know you're *really* mad, you're really insane!" So I guess I've just lived my life how I want to live it. And people around me, that's actually their problem. [Laughter]

Gretchen Dewitt

Public relations professional

I think most of us looked to our mothers. My mother helped me because she had such a love for Earth. She still does. I asked her recently if she was afraid of dying. She's seventy-five. And she said, "No, not at all, I'm not afraid of getting old. I'm not afraid of dying. But I think I'm an Earth person. I will not want to leave." And she helped me to appreciate the beauty of Earth.

She also helped me take risks. I grew up feeling that I didn't have to be afraid of anything. She told me I was smart and pretty and that I could do anything that I wanted to do. And she did not give me rules. She trusted me. She let me know that she expected me to be honest, so I was. And I give my mother a lot of credit for her example of loving life and having fun.

I went to school in Switzerland. When I was seventeen, my mother asked me, would I like to go to school in Switzerland. I said, "No, I really wouldn't like to go at all." She said, "Well, I have narrowed it down to three schools, and you'll be going." I knew that I would be missing my senior prom, and the beach, and boys, and I was not thrilled about going. But from that experience and others, I learned that children have to be forced sometimes to do things or they will never do them. Like going to the library, which I loved when I was forced to go, or taking dance lessons, which I didn't want to do.

So I went to Switzerland, and there I had a teacher named Jill Ruckleshaus. She was Jill something-else at the time, and she had just graduated from Vassar, I think. She was my English teacher. We were studying English literature, nineteenth-century, and poetry, and she would ask me what things meant. I always somehow knew what it meant. I felt smart, really smart, for the first time. And I credit her for telling me that I was, and for telling me that I could go to college and get all B's without any effort, but that I could be more than that—that I could decide what I wanted to be, because I could be whatever it was. I remember her for that. I blossomed in that year. I was with girls from all over the world, and it was a really loving school.

I remember my aunt, my mother's sister. I had a father who was rather a monster, an alcoholic, and not a kind person. My mother, thankfully, left him when I was very young. My aunt asked me once when I was in my early twenties, "Do you love your father?" I said, "No, I don't think I do." I'd always felt terrible about not really loving him. She said, "Do you feel bad about that?" I said, "Yes, I do. I feel like I should love him." And she said, "We love people because they are lovable. We love people because they're loving. We don't have to love people because they're related."

That freed me. I didn't feel guilt anymore about not loving my father. He was not lovable or loving. It also made me realize that for my children to love me, it wouldn't be enough for me just to be their mother, that I would have to be lovable and that I would have to be loving to them. So that was an important moment in my life.

Alice Waters
Restaurateur/Author/Educator

I had a lot of cooking mentors. And, of course, friends encouraged me.

I think having a network of friends is terribly important. I've always hired people who are friends to work with me. People sometimes say you shouldn't do that. But if I'm going to be with somebody for eight, ten, fifteen hours a day, I want it to be with somebody I like very much, rather than just somebody who can do the job.

Madeleine Albright
Former Secretary of State

My parents were fabulous people who did everything they could for their children and brought us to this amazing country and were protective, overly so in terms of worrying about us and all kinds of things. Because of my parents' love of democracy, we came to America after being driven twice from home in Czechoslovakia, first by Hitler and then by Stalin.

I am very proud of my family, of my parents, of what I believe in, what I have gotten—the honor of everything that has happened to me in the United States. All you have to do is read my speeches or talk to my friends or assess anything about my public life to know that I have always believed the Holocaust to be one of the great horrors of history. And actually I have to say that I'm very proud of the way I have lived my life. I think, if you look at my works, that I have comported myself in a way that is very much in line with somebody who has known repression and what it's like to be a victim of totalitarianism.

Rosie Casals
Professional athlete

Someone who influenced me was Billy Jean King. I remember when I first met her. It could have been 1961, 1962. I played doubles with her and Carol Gregner in Berkeley. I played with my girl-friend I've known forever, Gloria Cedarquist. We were a doubles team, and we played Carol and Billy Jean and lost, 6–3, 7–5.

I remember being so impressed with Billy Jean and Carol with their five rackets and their Fred Perry tennis skirts. They both looked immaculate with their beautiful, beautiful outfits. We're looking at them and thinking, "Wow, I want to be like them."

So that was the first time I met Billy Jean. Then I played her once again in 1963, in one of our tournaments in northern California. Then we started talking. She was going over to play Federation Cup in Italy, and she said, "Maybe we're going to play in the next year or two, when you go to Wimbledon. One of these days we'll play." And I kept in touch with her. We'd play against each other. Then, in 1966, she asked me to play with her. Mind you, she had just won Wimbledon in 1964 and in 1965 with another partner. So I thought, "Oh, wow." But she was a good mentor. She was someone who was very encouraging, very dedicated. So she played a very big role in my life.

We always have remained friends. Although many times we have been on the opposite side of the net, and on the opposite side of ideas and philosophies and things, we've still remained very close friends.

Leslie Young
Ballet soloist

Well, of course, my parents influenced me. Their encouragement has always inspired me. They supported me in what I loved to do. My poor mom drove me to ballet classes every day for years until I could go on my own.

My first ballet teacher was another influence. I think she's the one who instilled the love for dance and the aspect of discipline. I had an opportunity to go back and see how she is teaching the classes nowadays. It's very similar to what I remember. I mean, she made me laugh. She would show us that you had to be onstage, and you had to smile no matter what hurt, because you're performing for the audience. She said, then you run into the wing and that's when you can let it all out and breathe, and go: "Oh, my foot, my foot!" She'd say, "Then you come back out onstage, and you've got the greatest smile, and you bow and you say 'Thank you very much.'" She would act that out, and it made it all very real to me, and it made it fun, and it made it seem like the thing that I wanted to do: a little bit of pretend and play.

After we'd had our little performance in her studio, she would say, "Okay now, let's tell the audience (you know, it was all parents) what we did that was not so good today, what didn't go so well." And we'd have to say, "Well, I forgot this step" or "I fell down over in the corner." And she'd say, "Okay, now what did we do well?" So early on she instilled that balance of, it's okay to make mistakes and acknowledge them, but also acknowledge what you did well so that you're not heavy on one side or the other. You're not always beating yourself down. You're not pumping yourself up either. There's always that balance. So she influenced me a lot. And I've had other teachers along the way who have always put in their special moments of inspiration and keeping me going.

The other person is my husband, who keeps me going now. He often tells me that I've inspired him by doing something that I love to do. Like we said earlier, not everyone does what they like to do. And he has actually changed his career path. He is very involved in music. He loves music. He studies in conducting, and he is also a businessman who loves business. And he loves to sing. So we're able to communicate on that level. But it's funny, it inspires me that I can see that I've inspired someone else! And whenever I get nervous about a performance, or anxious, he says, "Now don't forget, you're a sharer; you're going to go out there and share your gifts. So just be calm and relax. This is what you rehearsed for, and this is what you love to do, so don't forget that."

Elizabeth Colton

Entrepreneur

I think I'm inspired by all of the women who went before me. I couldn't say that my hero is Susan B. Anthony or Eleanor

Roosevelt, although I certainly admire them greatly, but I think that as I work on this museum project, every day people tell me stories of the women that they have either read about or knew in their lives.

The other day I heard these stories about pilots in the Soviet Union called Night Witches, who went out and flew only at night. There are so many inspiring stories, from the woman who crossed the prairie in the wagon by herself, taking care of her five kids, to the women who were the pilots at night, to explorers. There are so many inspiring stories that I find myself surrounded by them more and more as I get into this project. I'm not an expert in women's history, so I'm learning a lot as we go along. There is so much. It's terribly exciting. For women's history there are actually a lot of resources out there now, but they're not very accessible. They're people's papers. There are academic books that aren't necessarily popular books. To be able to take on those stories and turn them into life in this museum is an extraordinary opportunity.

Annelies Atchley
Educator/Artist

You don't know who you are if you don't know other people. This isolation that we have in America right now: I'm going to listen to my CDs, I'm going to do this for myself. Me, me, me, me, me. And we can afford to be me. That's the problem. This "being me" is a side thing of capitalism. If you're in a poor society, you immediately know that you can't be "me" by yourself. As soon as you have to rely on other people to survive, you suddenly know who you are in a group and where you belong. We are a tribe. Nobody lives on an island, and the quicker we learn that, the better we are for each other.

Nancy Currie

Astronaut

It seems like everybody I've ever worked with very closely becomes a lifelong friend, because I throw myself entirely into what I'm doing, and include the people that I'm doing it with.

Military commanders played a role. For example, at Fort Rucker in Alabama, I was one of only two women out of probably around two hundred instructor pilots. Because this was in the early eighties, a lot of these guys had flown in Vietnam. They were very seasoned guys, and I was pretty young. But these commanders gave me opportunities to be in jobs that required a fairly high level of skill, and to have influence, in some aspects, over what impacted worldwide aviation operations in the army. I have to give them credit for giving me that opportunity, instead of somebody who had been around for fifteen or twenty years. They took me, someone with three or four years of experience and a female on top of it, and entrusted me with that. To this day, they come to my launches, and I always try to express how grateful I am to them for giving me that opportunity.

Rabbi Stacy Friedman
Rabbi

My family's a very matriarchal family. A lot of people have a hard time with Judaism because it's so patriarchal. I never knew that because we had all the daughters and my mother was much more involved with religion and Judaism than my father, so it was very matriarchal. My grandmother was a great Jewish spirit and my great-grandmothers before that. My mother and grandmother used to tell me all these stories from my great-grandmother and all of her wise sayings from the Bible and different Jewish books. So in many ways my mother and grandmother and great-grandmother and women in my family who were very strong religious and spiritual presences were these role models in my life. I think that if they had been born today, they would have been rabbis too. But they couldn't be rabbis then, so they did the most they could do within their sphere, and they would influence the men and the communities around them.

Even now my grandmother, who is very old, has all these pithy sayings she uses, all these things from the Talmud and Jewish law books and things. Their example to me out of their mouth was always a little bit of a Jewish recipe and some moral aspect about life: "You should treat people this way," or all these sorts of things. Always about helping other people and giving to the community and opening your home and things like that. So they were my inspirations.

In terms of role models there were other women who weren't necessarily Jewish or religious women, but great women influenced me more than any man. When I was little I used to read any biography I could read about women: Amelia Earhart, Helen Keller, Florence Nightingale. The men didn't interest me much. Men interest me, but they were not role models for me, even though, growing up, the only rabbis I knew for most of that time were men. But strong women, whether they were strong religious women or women who I saw who were politicians or heroes, were most influential to me. Men never did it for me.

Valerie Coleman Morris
Anchorwoman/TV personality

Someone who influenced me was my maternal grandmother, whom I called "Mud." I could not pronounce "mother" and so I called her "mudder," and the whole family did. I mention her especially because in much of my writing in stories for my *Family in Mind* program that I've done for CBS for so many years, I'll refer to her so that people know of her and her bottom-line kind of wisdom. My grandmother is the spiritual kind of person in my life.

Another influence was my professor of journalism at San Jose State. He was the person who said to me, "You will be professional from this point forward" and who told me why it was important. I don't know that he was thinking that explicitly. That was just what he encouraged his students to do and be. He instilled, very early on, the importance of being professional. Sometimes, when you're a student, you think, "No one's seeing this. It's just for my classmates, so I can screw it up." His point was, "Every time as a journalist, get ready to do something. From this day forward, if you do this, that's an audience that you as a professional will be addressing. You will then get into the habit of being professional. It will be your first and second nature." He instilled that in me. So he was important.

Sylvia Boorstein
Author/Educator/Lecturer

First of all, my parents never scolded me. I cannot remember my parents ever finding me lacking for anything. Once my mother caught me in the bathroom smoking a cigarette. That's the worst. She didn't say anything about it until much later, when she said to me in a casual way, "If you want to smoke in the house and not get caught, you have to leave the window open." I grew up with parents who never had a bad word about me, which I'm positive is the biggest gift anyone can give anybody.

I lived with my parents and my grandmother—my father's mother—who loved me terrifically. My father's mother was my principal caretaker. She had come from Europe in 1920 with my father, who was then nine years old. They had been separated from her husband, who had left ten years previously to get a job. Then the war broke out and she was nine years a refugee. But she was not a depressed woman. She came here, she made a life, she picked up with that husband, she raised my father. They were poverty-stricken people and yet cheerful.

Both my parents were working people, and she was the principal person who raised me. She took tremendously good care of me. I would say to her, "I'm not happy." You know, when you're a kid, some-times you're not happy. And she'd say, not in a mean way, "It's not writ-ten anywhere that you have to be happy all of the time." I think that is marvelous, fundamental dharma. It's not written anywhere that you're supposed to be happy all of the time. I think I learned something pro-found. Usually, when I point out my spiritual teachers, I put her first.

I had the good fortune of many good friends. I took a course in Eastern Religion from Mary Neill at Dominican College in 1972, which is when we became good friends. I took my first course in Buddhism from her, which is really sweet. She was a Catholic nun teaching a Jewish woman Buddhism that I will end up teaching all over the place. Mary and I became very fast friends. One of her teachings which I spread all over the world anytime I can comes from a time in Boulder when I was making a tape. Mary and I were going to teach a class together, and we were rushing out of my house to go teach and gathering up all of my books. We were a little late and I had this handful of books and we were rushing out the door and I said to her, "Wait a minute. I don't think I have everything I need." And she said, "Sweetheart, you're never going to have everything you need." So profound. It's exactly true. You're never going to have everything you need. Everything else is just a fantasy. So she is one of the great, wise women of my life.

All of my Buddhist teachers have tremendously informed my life. They were very important to me, as are my friends and teachers more recently in the Jewish community. All of my friends support me and inform me in my teaching. It's a gift.

I was on a panel of four or five teachers at a conference recently, and someone asked, "What's the most sustaining thing in your own spiritual practice?" I don't remember what everybody else said, but I said, "My friends."

Reverend Veronica Goines
Presbyterian pastor

Probably a number of people influenced me one way or another. I had a few childhood pastors, because my family moved around a little bit—my dad was in the navy. The childhood pastor I really claimed and had a connection with was Reverend Verdell Calhoun. Like many other people, he recognized something in me and encouraged it by always sending me to places where I would be exposed to teaching and to leadership development and training. It was as if I came through life and God placed people in my path who were able to see in me things I didn't consciously know myself at the time.

My mother declared her call to the ministry. It took five years before she was able to be ordained. She went through a lot of painful experiences because she was rejected in a lot of places. In the Baptist Church women were not ordained. Even when she was ordained in 1976, the pastor who ordained her and the ministers who formed the commission to ordain her were greatly ostracized. Still, she was one of the primary people. I wouldn't have said so at the time because I was dealing with my own struggles with that and what that meant. Also, the years of conditioning about the limitations of women in ministry took a lot to overcome.

Also my second marriage, in much the same way as my first, forced me to get some clarity about having some goals for my own life. It was like I had to have this clarity about my call, especially in the midst of what was a short but very painful experience. So that became a place for me where I had to learn how to be centered and grounded when everything was falling apart. It became a gift that has carried me for these last several years.

What I've encountered in life is that there's a lot of challenge, and sometimes it can come as a personal attack. So I have to find a way to be able to remain stable, constant, and centered in the midst of that. That experience really taught me the beginnings of how to do that and be clear about who I am and how precious I am and how worthy I am even when someone is saying otherwise.

There was a lot of inner development that I came to know, and a lot of change even in my theology. I think the flaws in my theology became very apparent. I had to look again at how I viewed God and how I viewed myself and come to a far more gracious interpretation of that relationship.

Marti McMahon

Entrepreneur

I must say that I have met people along the way in my business that I have been able to go [to] and ask for help, whether it is accounting issues or whether it is a naval architect that I need to explain how something can function on a boat. I think that what one has to do is to seek the people who know more than you do and ask for their help, because I think people are very, very willing to offer their advice. All you need to do is to ask and also be open to people who ask you for help. I've asked people to help me along the way, and they have turned around and in some way I have helped them.

Early on, when I was going through my financial crisis, we lost our family home. I remember very well when the judge put his fist down and said, "And the family home shall be sold to pay for all the bills." I thought I would even lose the little part of the business that I had. At that point in time, the business was grossing $200,000 a year, that was it. I thought I was going to lose even that. And there was a client that I had, who is still my friend today, and is still my client, who loaned me $50,000 just to keep afloat. I didn't want to take it, but he insisted, and I was finally at the point of desperation where I accepted it. I paid every single dime back to him. And one day he said, "Marti, you're going to make more money than I do one day." I don't think that's the case, because he's extremely successful, but at any rate I find that God does put people in your path. If you keep your eyes open, you'll find those people. Definitely go ask for help, because you can't do it alone.

Jo Hanson
Artist/Environmentalist

I have had so much help, it is impossible to describe all of it.

One thing is that I spoke of my family being a troubled one and how my relationship with my mother was awful. I realized as an adult that, actually, she was enormously helpful to me. She made a huge difference in my life, possibly as a model. Within the limitations of the circumstance she was in, in retrospect I see that she handled everything very responsibly and very ethically and was a model for doing. If it needs to be done, do it. If she wanted something done and nobody did it, she did it. If it was papering the wall, okay, and if it was something else, okay—she would do it. She was an accomplished craftsperson in a great range of crafts and a talented dressmaker. At the time when I was a child, I thought her colors were embarrassing because my peers would say, "Oh!" They'd think the colors were improper, and I'd take that on: "Blue doesn't go with green." But my mother was right. Her colors were wonderful. But I didn't know that until I grew up.

I've had countless friends who made great differences in my life, and every one is so individual that I can't generalize by saying just "Friends helped me a lot." When I was an early teenager or younger, my best friend's mother adopted me into her family in many ways. That was helpful to me because it was a different model than my own family. It was a model of a family that worked together well and were rather overt about loving each other and did things together and enjoyed it. That was very helpful to be included in that kind of family.

Mary Bitterman
President/CEO, public television

In terms of the question of who helped me, and who influenced me, it was very much my parents, who were incredibly wonderful people of very solid values, of great respect for others, of humility, always remembering who had assisted them in making the progress they made in their lives. My father always used to say, "If anyone says, I did it all myself, you know he or she is an idiot." There are those people who open doors of opportunity for you, and you must always be mindful of the gratitude that is appropriate to extend to all of those people, whether teachers, or family, friends, or relatives, or people that you met at different points in your life, who had some confidence in you, who gave you a chance. That's what makes a difference.

There can be the sense of doing everything on one's own. That really is a very narrow view, and I think it's more constructive to see how one's progress is definitely facilitated by the actions of others.

Sister Mary Neill
Nun/Author/Educator

I think friends look at you and they call forth things in you that you don't see at all, that you have never seen that you have. It's friends who have very much sustained my professional work, my outer work.

I think that women need a lot of confirmation. They need cheering on: "Yeah do it! Yeah, your way of doing it, that's really great!" Lawrence Vanderpost says to love perfection is another way of hating life, for life is not perfect. As nuns, the vows we took were called vows of perfection. So I have really struggled all my life with being a tremendous disappointment. And then I find that my friends love my imperfections. They think they are hysterical.

Again, you need people to give you confirmation. I think what women need to do is to ask for it. We are givers, but you have to receive as much as you give, and most of us are absolutely caught in spiritual malpractice. We think if we give and give and give that someone will look up and say, "You need rest and you need to receive," but that doesn't happen. So I think it's really important to cultivate friendship.

Friendship has just been absolutely central for me. It is a kind of astounding miracle to me what friends have done in my life, what they do.

Jeanne Rizzo
Entrepreneur

There are women who mentored me, who could recognize that I didn't have access to that mentoring in my home life and who could give it to me and challenge me. That had a tremendous influence.

Also great women I read about and who I saw making a difference out in the world—everybody from Bella Abzug to Eleanor Roosevelt—had an influence on me. Others, too. Martin Luther King. Gloria Steinem. The feminists. The antiwar activists. Those were people that I could see were doing the kind of work that made a difference on a grand scale.

Chapter 6

Turning Points

That was a turning point because what I made the decision
to do on that day was to not live my life as a victim anymore
but to begin to live my life very intentionally.

Reverend Veronica Goines

Many events in our lives become turning points. Something fundamental in our world shifts, and we are called upon to adapt and to grow, sometimes even to be reborn.

Though turning points may be happy surprises, often they are moments of crisis, of simultaneous danger and opportunity. They may be moments of loss, even of tragedy, and yet in each of them there is an opportunity to make new choices. This is the message I hear in the thoughts of the women in this chapter, who ultimately responded to change in a positive way and made even the most difficult situations occasions of growth.

Isabel Allende

Author

There have been many turning points in my life. My father's absence. My mother marrying my stepfather. Me meeting my first husband. I was fifteen, I met him and I fell in love, and my life changed. I come from a family where people don't touch. Something opened up for me the first time he touched me, the world of the senses, where I had never lived before, and that was crucial to my life. It turned me into a different person.

Some books that I read as a young woman gave me an articulate language to express the anger that I felt as a woman in a patriarchal society. I didn't know the word "feminist" at the time. But when I read those books, I confronted that word and realized I had always been a feminist. This was another turning point because it allowed me to work with a feminist perspective as a journalist, and from that time on all my life has been marked by feminists. That is important in my life because it determines my personality. I'm extremely independent, especially economically. I don't want anybody, let alone a man, to pay for anything that I need. I have always supported myself and my family. It's the consequence of the fact that I could not trust my father to support me, and then my feminism.

Another turning point was the military coup in Chile that forced me out of my country and made me a political animal. Today, although

I do not belong to any political party, I know that everything is politics, and I know that even if I do not participate I am, by my absence, participating in a negative way. So much of my effort goes to those causes, political causes, that I believe in. For example, education is something that is political, and I'm very involved in that. I have created a foundation to help people, especially women and girls from ethnic minorities, who don't have the money to get an education. All those things have come from the fact that I lived through a military coup and became aware of something that I was not aware of before.

Writing was another turning point. My divorce. Meeting Willie, my second husband. Moving to this country. And of course, the greatest of all—my daughter's death. I should not say that this was the greatest of all, because greater than her death was her birth. I was very young, nineteen, when I married. I was twenty when she was born. Motherhood changed me completely. I could never think of myself again as an individual. My daughter and my son and I are like a three-legged table. The fact that my daughter died doesn't make the table unstable. We are still three.

I think my son feels that way, too. She's very much of a presence. My two children were very, very close. They were uncomfortably close, because very often they would get together against me. Recently my son had to make a very important decision in his life. We had been talking about it. Then I traveled, and when I came back, he had a decision. I said, "I'm glad you made this decision. This is what I would have advised, and I didn't dare say it." He said, "You didn't have to. Paula did." I didn't ask how he got that answer from her, but she must be as present in his life as she is in that little chair in mine.

Lynn Woolsey

Congresswoman

Looking back at it, being a single mom and all that was a rebirth. It took many years to look back and say, "That was the beginning of Lynn Critchett, who became Lynn Woolsey. That was the beginning of Lynn." Up until then I was my mother's image of what a girl should be and this manic-depressive husband's image—or my image—of what a perfect wife and mother should be. Thirty years old, I got to be me. It was a horrible experience, but it was really good luck that I got that chance. I would be doing it now or sometime in my life, because I wasn't going to not be me forever. But I got thirty years of being able to be a real person.

Graduating from college was important to me. Certainly having my children. I consider them probably one of the greatest reasons that I stayed anchored and centered and humble. There's nothing more humbling than four teenagers who remind you daily of who you really are. That was an important turning point in my life.

A lot of steps I've taken in my life, I haven't known how scary they were until a couple of years later. When I left the electronics manufacturing company and started my own business, it wasn't until I was rethinking where that business was going to go two years later that I realized what a giant risk I had taken. Then going from city council to the House of Representatives—what a huge step that was. Had I known how little I knew both times, I probably would have had second thoughts. But I'm always going forward. I seldom go back. My greatest weakness is I hate process. I just hate process. So I don't go through the

"Should I or shouldn't I?" I really trust my gut on a lot of stuff, and it's usually right.

Carmel Greenwood
Entrepreneur

When I was in Hong Kong, the more successful I got, the more my husband was angry. He got jealous; he said I was having affairs. So one night I came home and he tried to strangle me. I think that night I left my body. I saw my body lying on the floor, and I realized that I had to leave. He always blackmailed me, saying that he would see me in the gutter where I belonged. So I left. I walked out the door with my Buddha, and that's all I took . . .

My first husband trying to strangle me was a major turning point because I realized that I didn't have to be a victim of life anymore. When I saw my body lying on the floor, I realized that if I walked out the door, I would not be financially secure, but what I would have with me was my dignity. And my consciousness.

I could also always re-create money. But my dignity was the most important. That was what shifted, and I realized that I would never allow anyone to abuse me ever again.

Gretchen Dewitt
Public relations professional

Falling in love for the first time is a turning point for most people. I was surprised by love. I didn't know what love was. I was twenty-one, and I had spent from the age of I would say fourteen or fifteen kissing lots of cute boys, nothing else but kissing. It was an innocent time. I don't know how often I had spoken to these boys about anything. I danced with them, I kissed them, went to movies with them. I think I did all my talking with my girlfriends. Boys were for kissing and dancing, and, I guess, paying for the movie. So I had never had a serious heartthrob.

I was going to school in Mexico City my junior year of college, and a tall blond American—he was six-four, and in school—walked up to me and said, "I understand you're a Mormon." I said, "Yes I am." And I don't know why I said this, but I said, "And that means I don't drink, or smoke, or even fool around." So he said, "Well, would you go out to dinner with me?" I said, "Yes, I would." My allowance was never big enough, and I was dying to be taken out to dinner.

So we went out to dinner and talked. Then one night—we had been out three times and talked a lot each time—we were driving through Chapultapec Park, and he asked me if he could hold my hand, and I said yes, he could. Then, when we got to the front gate of the home where I was living with a Mexican family, he asked if he could kiss me good night, and I said yes, he could. And he gave me the best kiss of my life. He asked if I'd like to go inside, and I said, no, I wouldn't. So we kissed for hours, literally, and I remember hearing bells at one point, and I thought, "Oh, this is really love." And I opened my eyes up, and it was dawn and the milkman was arriving with his little bicycle and ringing the bell, delivering the milk.

So I fell in love with this person. And what changed then was that I had always felt that I was in control, that I was the one in charge, and now I wasn't. And he was leaving, he graduated and was going back. I remember having dinner with him at the Normandy Club in Mexico City, and looking at him when we were talking, and thinking, "My throat is aching so much. What is the matter with my throat?" It hurt me. And I thought, "Oh my gosh, I'm going to start crying. Something's terribly the matter here." So I ran off to the ladies' room and spent about fifteen minutes sobbing. And I knew I was in love and that I was not in control of my feelings, that I wasn't in charge, that love was in charge. That changed my life at that moment. I had lost control and lost my being-in-charge status.

Falling in love was a shift, and it scared me, so I don't know if that was to my advantage at the moment. I was afraid of love because I didn't know what was going to happen to my advantage. Ultimately, to fall in love or to love is always to one's advantage, because it expands the heart. The heart gets bigger, so it's always an advantage to experience love. To not experience love is a great disadvantage.

Rosie Casals
Professional athlete

A *turning point in my life* was when I first was introduced to tennis, when I realized that there was a career for me. I probably was about eighteen, nineteen. We turned professional, Billy Jean, myself, Frankie Gear, Ann Jones. We turned pro with Rod Laver, Poncho Gonzales, Ken Rosewall, Andre Semenes. We signed our contract with the National Tennis League, and that's the first time we'd ever made money.

We were very much ostracized by the other women tennis players, because we were told we were just playing tennis for the money. I was very much like Billy Jean in that I believed things had to change because players were getting paid under the table. We knew there was money out there, so why wouldn't we declare it? Otherwise we were just being hypocritical when tournaments and promoters and what have you were paying money under the table for specific players.

So we took the big bold step and decided that we were going to turn pro. Our first month we must have played thirty days in a row in Europe. We played in the south of France to audiences of probably two hundred and three hundred people because pros were not well known in regard to being pros. The names were well known, but not the tour. And although Laver and Rosewall had been doing this for ten years, with Jack Kramer being one of the promoters in the very beginning of the professional tour, it was still very, very different and unacceptable for women to be pros.

So we played at odd times and odd places. We had thought that when we turned pro, things were going to be great. We'd stay at the five-star hotels because we had money and all that. We really had a rude awakening. It was hard work. It was dedication, and all of us were very dedicated to the game.

That was one of the greatest moments in my life because here was Laver, who'd won Wimbledon, a Grand Slam. Here were Ken

Rosewall, Poncho Gonzales—I mean the legends of tennis. And they were talking to us, they were helping us with our game. We traveled with them. We watched them play. We learned so much about them, about the game, which really helped us.

The next step was to go our separate ways from the way tennis had been with the men and women, to take the bold step against the establishment and establish our own tour. Players such as Ann Jones and Frankie Geret, Billy Jean, and myself, were very instrumental in making that change. We were kind of given the cold shoulder by the Margaret Courts and the Virginia Wades, and ultimately the Chris Everts, who went against our tour. They didn't understand; they thought we were doing it just for the money. We were doing it to put women's tennis on the map and to be able to say that it's okay for women to want to play a sport.

At that time there wasn't a Title IX, so women were not given scholarships to pursue any sports whatsoever. We started our Virginia Slims tour in 1970, with the first tournament being in Houston, which I won, and that was the first time that women played on their own, basically separate from the men.

Leslie Young
Ballet soloist

I guess the main turning point for me was dancing to a violin concerto. I had a pas de deux to do, and the woman who came to set the piece said, "You know, these steps are very simple, and it's up to you to make them into something beautiful or something interesting." The music was Stravinsky, which is already quite intricate, and here was someone who said, "Here you go. Do something with it." And it was hard. It was very hard, because I was used to having people tell me exactly what to do. When you're in the corps, you're told exactly how high your leg is, you know where you look at a certain count. It scared me a bit at first, and then the more I got to do it, the more freedom I had, the more interesting and vulnerable I became to people around me, because I would experiment to see how far I could push this line in my body. "Oh, listen, there's an instrument that I didn't hear that time. What happens if I emphasize that instrument there, so I that I try and let the audience hear something new?" There were all these different aspects of the dance itself, and of the music, and I loved it.

I think that was probably the turning point for me, to be given all that freedom. I really loved that. When you see *Swan Lake*, you see twenty-four girls all dressed in white, and they are all the same. Their legs are all the same level; they are all doing the same step; they are all dressed exactly alike. That's part of the beauty of it, that there are twenty-four girls moving as one. But you don't have a unique voice in a situation like that. Your concentration and focus are on being like everyone else. I think it took a bit of time to be given the opportunities and to find that I did have a unique voice. I could do a step and make it look different than someone else doing the same step. It goes back to that idea of freedom within a structure. It's the same step, which is the structure, but the way I'd execute it, compared to the way someone else would execute it, could make it look completely different. There's that freedom within the structure.

I think that was a major turning point in realizing that I had a voice and that someone had listened to it and encouraged it. In that time right before I was promoted, I was given opportunities to speak, to explore and see what I came up with, to reach down deep into my soul and see what was there and bring it up and show people, which is a hard thing to do. It makes you very vulnerable when you put yourself out on the line and see how people respond.

That was a maturing time in my life. It was a new way of seeing things. When I would perform as a student or in the early years, I would see people in the wings watching while I was out on stage, and I would always be afraid that those people were judging me. For some people, that makes them feel like "I'm going to prove it to you." But, for me, it made me feel insecure. It was a fear that I had. I didn't really want people I knew to come see me dance. Then all of a sudden I thought, "Well, if I have this voice, I'm going to use it and I'm going to share." And all of a sudden I was seeing people who came to see me as friends, and I wanted them there because they were supporting me. I realized that they weren't judging me. They wanted to hear what I had to say. They wanted to see how I danced. They were enjoying these gifts that I was trying to give to the audience.

Elizabeth Colton

Entrepreneur

My divorce was a turning point. Not to demean the man who was my husband, but for me it was a liberating time. It was an occasion to be able to find myself and find my place in life, if you will, and make a contribution as myself.

Throughout this recent time [working on the museum project], there have been a lot of little successes—the first draft of our document, when you could read it and see that it was really important; or the first check that we got for a thousand dollars; or the first time I met with a high-ranking official who said "Absolutely."

I would say recently that the moments are a collection of smaller moments when I am finding that there are a lot of people out there who really believe in this project and who I think will help me make it happen. That keeps me going, the fact that this is so universally accepted. Not just accepted but—I can't explain it. The faces of women when I start telling them about this project . . . it's incredible and keeps me going every day.

Rabbi Stacy Friedman
Rabbi

I had a lot of changes and moves and a lot of turning points in my life. The first was moving to Utah as a young teen. Before that I had lived in New York, which was predominantly Jewish. There, being Jewish or being part of a religious community was something that was very natural and a given, but not something that people necessarily worked hard at in my general surroundings. In Utah, being religiously involved was of primary importance. That was a whole new outlook and a whole new way of life for me. Until we moved to Utah, being

Jewish and being involved with community was very important, but it wasn't the central feature of my life. Once I moved to Utah, it was. It was imposed by the outside, but it was something that my family took on very naturally.

Living in Israel was also very influential to me because when I lived in Utah I really felt like an outsider for the first time. I felt that I looked different and I was different. Not that people weren't perfectly nice to me and I didn't have good friends, but I felt like an outsider. I remember that when I was in Israel the first time after a period of time that I didn't live there, I felt instantly very, very natural. I had curly hair like everybody else, and I fit in and I loved speaking Hebrew, and it feels like it just fit my emotions.

I remember seeing a boy who lived down the street from me in Utah walking down a central street in Jerusalem, and I looked at him and thought: "He looks so out of place. He looked so in place in Utah, and there I looked out of place." Not that I didn't wish him well, but it felt so good that I was in my homeland, and I thought that was a wonderful thing.

It was a real turning point for me to see that Judaism was something that could be lived any moment of life. The cycle and rhythm of life in Israel are the cycle and rhythm of life of the Jewish people. Here, when the Sabbath for me is Saturday and there are all of these things that go on on Saturday, it's hard to make that happen. But in Israel, Friday afternoon everything stops. There are no buses Saturday, the stores are closed. I don't have to fight to get the Jewish holidays off or wonder what I'm going to do on Christmas when everybody else is with their families. So that was really a turning point for me in terms of my comfort and realizing how much Judaism could be a rhythm that I have in my life. It's not the only rhythm, but it's an important one.

Sylvia Boorstein
Author/Educator/Lecturer

Probably a turning point was the death of my mother when I was twenty-three. I had anticipated it in some way all of my life because my mother had rheumatic heart disease. She didn't have the stamina and fortitude and health that other people's mothers did. She was bedridden and not in pain, but I knew that she was frail and I knew that her health was compromised. I worried probably excessively when I was younger that she might die at any moment. People don't usually die at any moment of those kinds of heart troubles, but she died when I was twenty-three. I had been married five years and had two children by that time and was happy, but her death served to get through to me on some level that we will lose everyone who is dear to us if they don't lose us first. I think it was one of my most dramatic wake-up calls to the existential, frail nature of our experience. If I had had the breadth of knowledge at the time to say I was having a crisis of existential angst I would have said it, but I didn't know how to say it that way. I just got frightened.

About five years later I had the good fortune to be able to address some of those fears in psychotherapy. Fears don't entirely get addressed in psychotherapy, but we get to see the patterns that keep us un-free or constrained now in our relationships—repeating, debilitating habits. In addition, what therapy did not do for me, which I did not know until much later, was something I discovered as a result of my spiritual practice. There's a way in which the wounds of our lives become more healed in the context of a kind of contented, relaxed, trustful, or faithful mind that is a gift of our religious practice. There's a certain healing that takes place just in the context of that altered space of connection with a bigger reality than the small one of our particular, personal story.

The other piece of religious or spiritual practice that I find sustaining is the trust that any of us, regardless of what's going on, can at least sometimes touch that way of being that says, "Life itself is okay. My life at this point is very difficult, but life itself is not a mistake. It's all right and there will be times again when my sense of the allrightness of life will be enough so that my life in the middle of it will also be enough no matter what it is."

Reverend Veronica Goines
Presbyterian pastor

My bed is really where a lot of stuff happens in the way of my spiritual journey. It was seven and a half years before I acknowledged my call that I was sitting at the foot of my bed. My two children were very young at this time. It was such a powerful time—I was at the point that I was so into this sense of being so inadequate and just suffering with my self-esteem and feeling like I didn't know how to give my children what they needed. In fact, they were getting everything they needed, but it was just my own stuff that was in the way. It had become so pervasive for me that I remember sitting on the bed and just crying out to God and saying, "God, I can't do this. I just give up. I just need to give up." I asked God to take me home. I didn't want to be here anymore, and I was trying to really bargain with God about who would be able to take care of my children. I never thought about suicide, I just wanted God to sweep in and pick me up and carry me home. [Laughter]

Of course, that didn't happen, but the thing is I was able to cry out to God and really be so open about what I was feeling. But I couldn't see my way clear to work through those feelings. I picked up the phone and was going to call this counseling service, but instead I prayed and talked to God about it. What I heard God say was not to give up but to give it up to God, to actually surrender this to God.

I had my hands up, literally, like I was surrendering this whole situation, and this peace just began to reenter my life. That was a turning point because what I made the decision to do on that day was to not live my life as a victim anymore but to begin to live my life very intentionally. That was the point that led into my career change into the graphics field, and things began to blossom from there.

Irene Zisblatt Zeigelstein
Holocaust survivor

When we arrived at the camp, they ordered the men to stay behind and the women and children to come off the train. Nobody wanted to come off the train without their families, and so they said, "The men will come later, and they will bring your suitcases. You need to leave your suitcases."

My mother had sewn four diamonds into my skirt. They had told us that we were going to work in this vineyard, so she told me before we left on the cattle train that in case we had to work in separate places and they didn't give me enough food to use those diamonds to buy bread with because they would be like money. So I had them in the skirt, and when we left all of the suitcases, of course, that's all we had, the clothes on our body.

When we got to the platform, there was someone who was kind of directing traffic, pointing who goes where. My mother took my brother and she held him in her arms and then she held my sister by her hand, and I was holding on to my sister so we shouldn't get separated by the shoving and the pushing. Then we reached the platform and the mothers were being separated from their children, sisters from sisters, and it was like chaos, pushing and shoving, and this man ordered my mother to put the children down, because, God knows, he didn't want to save any children. My mother wouldn't obey him, and she held on to the children and she told me, "Hang on tight." She told him she would not leave her children, and he got angry . . . He separated me from my sister with this rubber baton. I have a spot on my hand even today from that. He pushed me in the opposite direction from my mother and the children, and I immediately had this feeling that he was punishing my mother for not obeying him, so he was taking me away from her anyway. I started to scream. I wanted to go with my mother. And the harder I screamed, the faster they were pushing me away from her. Then I heard her in the distance, she called out to me, "Don't cry, don't cry. I will come later and get you." Then she and her voice just disappeared in the distance. Then I thought of my father being with my brothers in the train, so I started running toward the train, to go find my father, and they took me and they shoved me into a convoy of people that I had never seen before.

Before you know it, we were in this big tremendous building . . . The loudspeaker was yelling orders, and they ordered us to take our clothes off and hold our clothes in one hand and our shoes in the other. I remembered the diamonds in the skirt, so I quickly took the diamonds out of the skirt and I had nowhere to put them, so I put them in my mouth. Then we had to drop the shoes in one bin and the clothes in the other bin, and they kept directing us toward a next station, and all the time they were announcing, "If you have any valuables, drop them in another section." I had the diamonds in my mouth and I thought, "I'm not going to give these diamonds up, because my mother said I have to buy bread with them, and these are her diamonds and I cannot give them up." And I held them in my mouth until I got to the station where I saw they were opening up people's mouths in front of me and they were extracting gold fillings and gold teeth, and I said, "Oh my God! The diamonds in my mouth, they are going to open my mouth and they are going to see the diamonds and they are going to shoot me." There was no place I could put them, because I was naked. So, in a fit of panic, I swallowed them, and then I felt, "Well, they can't get them unless they cut my stomach open, but they do not know they are in there."

Then they shaved my head, they examined my mouth, and then they put us into another room and we saw showers, so we thought we were going to get showers, but the showers never came on. Instead they came in with the hose, and they hosed us down with this white stuff and they said this was disinfectant powder and that was the same as a shower. There was a pile of clothes by the door, and they ordered us to take one piece of clothing, no matter what it was—a pajama top, a pajama bottom, a blouse, or a dress, or whatever it was, that's what you were stuck with. They gave us no shoes.

This huge mirror was by the door, and as we were passing we couldn't help but see ourselves in this mirror, it was put there on purpose, and I saw myself in the mirror and I said, "Oh my God! My mother will never recognize me. She will not find me because I don't look like I'm supposed to be looking." I started to cry, and everyone was yelling at me, "Stop crying because we're all going to be shot." I was the youngest one in the group, you know, and everybody was trying to take care of me, but I was so upset that I couldn't stop crying.

Then in the courtyard, as they were lining us up five across, I looked over to the next courtyard and in the distance I saw my mother and the children and my father and my brothers, and they were walking down a ramp into a little house. I said, "Oh great, that is where they are going, and then later my mother is going to come get me and we are all going to live in this little house." What I found out later was that that little house was the gas chamber. But I didn't know.

They processed us into the camp and put us in a barrack, one thousand people into a barrack, ten people in a bunk bed. By the end of the day my mother didn't show up, so I got off my bunk bed and went to the door to see if maybe I could see her because I knew she wasn't going to find me looking like I was. The head of the block, the barrack, came out from her little room and said, "Where do you think you're going?" I said, "I'm going outside to see if my mother is here because she is supposed to come get me and they shaved my head and they took my clothes away and I don't know whether she is going to find me, so I'm going to look for her." She grabbed me by the collar and pushed me out the door, and she pointed to six chimneys in the distance and she said, "See that chimney over there? That's where your mother is coming out just about now. You're going to join her there in three months. And if you don't go back to your barrack, I'm going to escort you myself there right now."

I didn't know what she was talking about, and I went back to my bunk and the women in my bunk. I said, "Why is she saying that to me? This is terrible." And a woman said, "She is telling you the truth. Your mother is not going to come get you, and I hope that your mother is not in that chimney, but most likely all of our mothers are."

I can't say I survived because of a certain thing. There were many, many things that contributed to my survival. Like my mother's diamonds. I kept swallowing the diamonds through the whole time I was in the camp, and I retrieved them in the latrine. I still have them today. It would have been very easy to throw those diamonds away after I found out that I couldn't buy bread, but they became a reason for me to live another day. I had to hide the diamonds or I had to find the diamonds. They were my mother's diamonds. I needed to take care of them. That was another reason for me to fight for life, I thought, and I survived with the diamonds. I have them today.

Jo Hanson

Artist/Environmentalist

Most of my turning points were traumatic, I would say, and most of them were invaluable to me.

I guess it was a turning point when I decided to get married because I considered that I wouldn't. It was a turning point when I decided to have children because I had considered that I wouldn't.

I think possibly the first really enormous thing in my life was analysis, and that was precipitated by the fact that I was becoming characterologically so angry that even I knew it. I always thought it was the other guys. I was very fortunate in that I had an analyst who did not tell me what anything meant. The only role he took was asking a question if he thought I was missing something, and being present.

Analysis sets up experiences for really reliving things so that it changes the dynamic. It's not an intellectual process but a process of reexperiencing in another context. It was in analysis that I discovered that I was meant to be an artist.

Going back to art school was a turning point. I studied and was scared to death. Being an older person, I thought I would really be ostracized and looked down upon. The other students were so supportive and so marvelous that it was revelation, and it made a great difference to me.

The students were better than the faculty at that time, although faculties have changed. At that time, faculties were mainly men, and that was rough terrain. I encountered some men who were very helpful and many who were destructive . . .

A turning point was injuring my back terribly, which compelled me into situations where I discovered what I now call spirituality. I went to a chiropractor. He really saved me for several years until I became fully operative. He told me to go to yoga class, and I would find myself sitting in yoga class and I'd start crying. There was nothing about the class that was sad, and there was nothing that explained crying. I came to realize and understand that this was sort of a tissue response to a natural process of getting in touch with my own body, my own cells and organs.

That was the beginning of a further process of developing a spiritual understanding of existence and of what I was doing as an artist and what was meaningful to me as a person. Then I actually took classes in a spiritual system, and this was really a turning point—going into something I had always regarded as phony and fake and ridiculous. I was very much a science person. To become involved in what I then regarded as so ridiculous was quite a step.

Mary Bitterman

President/CEO, public television

I fully expected that after I did my PhD in modern European history at Bryn Mawr I would spend all of my adult life teaching and doing research on European subjects. When I finished my dissertation, my husband, a neurobiologist, was asked to be a visiting professor at the University of Hawaii. We were going to go for just a year. But we didn't stay for just a year, we decided to stay forever. So I have really spent, outside of these five years at KQED, all of my adult life since doing my graduate work in Hawaii, a society which has no majority group, a society where over seventy percent of the people trace their ancestry to the Asia-Pacific region. This caused me to become so interested and committed to the Pacific that I set my European studies aside and began to become hugely engaged in the study of Asian language, culture, communication systems, and the rest of it.

I was offered an opportunity, through various odd circumstances, to head the public broadcasting network in Hawaii, the only woman and the youngest person to head a public broadcasting center in the United States. It probably couldn't have happened any place else in the country except Hawaii, and because of a given set of circumstances and the close association that I was able to enjoy with people from every walk of life there, with the mentorship of Senator Daniel K. Inouye and the great confidence that I enjoyed from Governor George Arioshi, in whose cabinet I sat. These were all turning points in my life, which might have gone on to European studies, but instead moved in the direction of Asia. Instead of history it became communication, instead of a scholarly bent, a much more public service, public manager kind of role.

So it was really the move to Hawaii, I think, and all of the circumstances there and the influence of my colleagues and the entire Asian-Pacific tradition, that really did so much to expand my outlook, to increase the facets I've been able to see in every aspect of life. And this certainly redounded to my benefit. To feel oneself a citizen of a larger world is probably the most enfranchising experience you can have. Opportunities like those that I've had to live in Hawaii, to be a director of our nation's international radio service, to be able to travel broadly because of the nature of my work, to feel at home in so many different parts of the world, really give a sense of personal joy and strength which sees you through even the most difficult of times, and I think allows you to maintain perspective and, in fact, a joyful spirit.

Jeanne Rizzo

Entrepreneur

I think there are a couple of turning points that stand out for me. The first was having my son. I had already taken in my husband's two children as stepkids. That was certainly a turning point as well, but I found having my own child to be the most liberating experience as a woman. A lot of people see it differently. I felt that I fully understood and appreciated the full sense of myself as a woman on the planet and that I would not be the same again and that I also had an accountability that shifted. A true accountability. An unequivocal love that would change my life. I felt that that was very positive.

Up until that point, whenever anything would be hard for me, I would say, "Well what's the worst that could happen? The worst that could happen is that I could be poor. Well, I've been poor. The worst that could happen is that I could die. Well, so . . . ?" I always had that expression. After I had my son, I began to think in terms of what's the *best* that could happen? Because not being alive on this planet with him through his adulthood was so unthinkable to me that I had to change my paradigm. I had to actually confront it and say, "I can't think anymore about what's the worst that could happen. I now need to think about what's the best that could happen."

I felt challenged somehow having a boy child on this earth. I had always thought I wanted a girl child because I'm a feminist, but I realized that the real challenge is to bring that model to the young men on the planet and help shape or change just one person's way of thinking about women on the Earth, and I had that opportunity. So that was the best way that could happen. I think that was a defining moment for me . . .

The second turning point came when I had a head-on collision on the Golden Gate Bridge. I was hit by a drunk driver in 1987, and I had brain injury as well as body problems. That was a defining moment for me because I really left my body, I saw myself from above the bridge, and I recognized that I had passed over and back. That was an incredible moment for me, to have the gift of coming back, because I do believe that I left my body and there was a moment at which I might not have survived that. Coming back from the physical part of it, the spiritual shakeup that I went through and then literally the brain damage—having to rehabilitate myself—was a life-changing moment for me, when I really took stock of how I was going to live my everyday life. We were very successful, we had a thriving business, I was running five companies, I was a working parent; I was doing it all. So then I had to take stock and say, "I really need to regroup here and think about those things that I always said were important to me, yet I'm not living them." So those two moments are the two most crucial events for me.

Chapter 7

Following Your Bliss

I just love life. I just can't forget that I am alive and I make
every day meaningful and full because I feel it might be my
last . . . To appreciate life itself—that is a message that many
people need.

Irene Zisblatt Zeigelstein

Happiness is an elusive concept. We speak of the "pursuit of happiness," and yet, as Aristotle said, happiness is like the blush
on a runner's cheek. It is not something we can pursue directly, but
rather a by-product of doing what we love to do.

The women I spoke with are passionate about many things. When
I asked them about their happiest moments, the answers sometimes
focused on their life's work, sometimes on memorable times with their
parents and children, and sometimes on simple enjoyment of each
passing day. If there is a single message in this chapter, perhaps it is a
modern version of what Aristotle said long ago: Happiness means

enjoying the process—the being, the living, the doing, as we follow our bliss wherever it takes us.

Isabel Allende
Author

The happiest moments in my life? Motherhood is the happiest. Some encounters and some moments with men that I have loved passionately. Writing. The moments of writing. All the moments when I write, even the painful ones when I'm crying as I write, I love it. Nature. Moments in nature. Walking in the woods. Being in touch with nature is what has saved me from the darkest moments of depression. Every time I've been really down, going out and being in nature has helped.

Lynn Woolsey
Congresswoman

Having my children —all three of them, and I have a stepson, which is why I talk about four. But I gave birth to three children. That was a joy. I thought I just wanted to have sons, but when my daughter, who is my youngest, was born and the doctor told me she was a girl, I had no idea how much I wanted a daughter. I'm so glad I had her. She's such a good friend.

Graduating from college in 1982 and finalizing my degree—one of my sons then said he'd never seen me happier. He was a college kid then. That was such a good feeling.

I suppose being a member of Congress. That's a job, but it's a great job. That's my third biggest thrill in life.

Carmel Greenwood
Entrepreneur

You can be inspired to follow your dream and follow your bliss, and your heart knows. Follow your bliss. If your heart sings, go for it. If your heart doesn't sing, delete it. If I'm in bliss, then I do it. If I'm miserable, I walk out that door. I've walked out from dinner parties. If I'm not happy, I walk out. I don't have to make excuses for anyone. I just do it.

Gretchen Dewitt
Public relations professional

Before I married my first husband, I had had an autoimmune hemolytic anemia. It was a self-destruction of red blood cells. So I was very sick. I could barely lift up my head. I had lost eighty percent of my red blood cells. I was scared because I was in my mid-twenties and I was hospitalized, and I could not have surgery because to have the spleen removed, to have any kind of surgery, you have to have a hemoglobin count of ten, and mine was four. It had gone from fourteen to four.

I was having my blood taken three times a day. When I was scared, my blood count would go down. I was at risk to die; I could have caught anything. I had no immune system working and my blood cells were devouring each other, and no one knew why. There was another girl in the hospital who was in her twenties, and she had just died of the same disease.

But when I prayed, and when I felt strong in that I would be all right, my blood count would go up. I could tell every time. The doctor would come in and I would say it's going to be up or down. I was right every time. I would know when it was up and when it was down.

At this point I was going out with a man, a widower with four children. My mother was bringing in wedding dresses for me to try on, and of course, I couldn't even get out of bed. I thought, "Oh, this is so great. I look like a poor little ghost in bed, and she's bringing wedding dresses."

I married him several months after I got out of the hospital. I was on massive doses of cortisone, which stimulates red cell growth. The doctor did not tell me that this causes temporary sterility. I was only told not to get pregnant for the first year because I was on medication and that would be a problem for any developing fetus. So I did not. After the year was up, I asked my doctor if I could get pregnant. "Yes, you can now." I tried for a year, and of course, I couldn't get pregnant because of the residue of cortisone in my body. I was taking my temperature all the time, and pushing my husband into the bedroom every day, and depleting his sperm supply probably.

So one day I went in for a pregnancy test. I was late for my period, and I was convinced that I had induced this sort of false pregnancy, that I wasn't really pregnant. To pass the hours waiting for the results on the pregnancy test, I think I went to have my hair cut, and my nails done. I was too embarrassed to call the doctor myself, and I asked my husband if he would call for me.

I remember my husband picked me up in front of I. Magnin's. I got in the car. I was too afraid to ask him if I was pregnant. And he said, "Well, you're pregnant." And I embraced myself. I remember putting my arms around myself. That baby became a baby instantly and was my baby. The marriage wasn't the sort of marriage where it was our baby. It wasn't a strong, happy marriage. He was an alcoholic. I had married someone like my father, with four children. So it wasn't something I felt that I was having with him. I felt this was mine. And that was one of my happiest moments, because I had a baby.

Feeling the baby for the first time fluttering against me was another of my happiest moments. I don't think labor was one of my happiest moments. That was a bad three and a half hours. I kept thinking how anxious I had been to have this baby, and yet when I was in labor I thought, "Please, God, I'll be pregnant forever. Let's have this stop. I'll just go back to keeping this baby inside me."

Having the baby, to have that baby put on my belly, that was the happiest moment of all, because I felt that I'd run the marathon, that I had done everything, and I was the victor, I was the champion. I was thrilled. I can't think of a happier moment than that for me, and I've had many, many happy moments. But that for me is unbeatable.

Having a baby is what it's all about. This is what I was born for.

This is, you know, a divine pact, and it is something that is so basic. The heart beating almost instantly, the brain and soul, everything there. It's a real partnership with the divine. I think it's a very godlike act.

Alice Waters

Restaurateur/Author/Educator

Certainly times with my kid are among my happiest moments. And also the satisfaction of having people do things that you couldn't imagine. You think that they're at the limit of their capabilities, or you imagine their work in a certain way, and then they go way beyond that. It's very exciting to be involved in something like that, where there's something greater than the sum of the parts.

I was involved with this AIDS benefit a couple of years ago with restaurant people and artists and musicians and businesspeople. I just couldn't imagine how it was all going to come together. And people put forth this kind of effort that was way beyond. I didn't even learn about parts of it until after it was all over and I would see these beautiful boxes that they'd made, or menus they'd invented. It was just thrilling.

I like working with people, a whole group of people, to come up with something. Where I have my part, where I know how I fit, and we make something that nobody can imagine.

Rosie Casals

Professional athlete

I think one of my happiest moments was winning that first Virginia Slims tournament, when other women players were taking that giant leap, not knowing what was going to happen to us. Those were exciting moments that I wouldn't change. People say, "Look at all the prize money that the players are making now." I'd like their money, but I would not change the time, because it was special. The friendship with those players was special, Billy Jean and Frankie Gear and Ann Jones and Kerrie Reed, and the other players that took the risk for women's tennis—Nancy Ritchie, Fuchas Barkowitz, Christie Pigeon, Judy Dalton. They were very special individuals who wanted more for the game, wanted more for themselves, and saw the vision and took the chance.

We didn't know what would happen. The minute we did this and became pros, the United States Tennis Association and all the federations and their respective players said, "You can no longer play in any of the tournaments." There we were. We'd made this move, and now we had no place to play because we couldn't play Wimbledon, we couldn't play the U.S. Open. They said, "We're banning you." Fortunately, a month later they changed their mind and realized that things were changing and that they needed to change.

So they started this tour in competition with us, run by the United States Tennis Association, where Virginia Wade played Margaret Court, Chris Evert, and several of the other players. So we had two tours running. Those were very difficult times, because instead of dividing with the men here and the women there, the women divided one more time. So it was a scary time, but we finally did a good job of convincing the rest of the players that the tour they needed to be on was on the Virginia Slims.

And I've got to hand it to Virginia Slims. They spent millions of dollars putting women on the map. Eventually the operators of the other tour realized they could not compete with Virginia Slims; nor were they willing to put in the kind of money that Virginia Slims was. So they said "Okay, we're not going to fight with you guys. Go ahead, run the tour. You seem to be doing a good job." And from there all the way through 1977, 1978, we were golden.

Leslie Young
Ballet soloist

My wedding day! Actually there's this one moment, and I laugh because I just burst into tears over it. We got married at Grace Cathedral. They have these big bronze doors, two doors. They are not always open, but as a gift from the Cathedral, they opened them for us. So when we were walking up the aisle afterward for the recessional, those big doors were just opening. And here I am starting a new life with my husband and the doors are opening and this air is coming in and the music is playing in the background and we're supported by all these people on either side of us that came to see us get married, and it was just too much for me.

Elizabeth Colton

Entrepreneur

There are all kinds of ways to measure happiness. Recently, bringing this museum project to fruition is ecstatic — every time somebody says, "I'll do this for you. I support you." It's very rewarding.

But there are all kinds of happy moments. I got a report card from my son, who is fifteen. For the first time his report card said he's really doing better and he's really trying. He's a smart kid who hasn't really been trying that hard. At that moment to get that report that he is actually trying, that was a happy moment. So some kinds of happiness are tied up in the accomplishments of your kids or the love you get back from them.

Traveling. I love to travel and visit new places and to bring my children to have them experience the world and different cultures and communities. So there are many different levels of happiness, from the personal to the professional. The personal comes, really, through my kids, and the professional and the inspirational happiness comes from the successes of this project.

Sue Backman

Entrepreneur/Billiards professional

As far as times I remember crying because I was so happy, I guess almost all of those are experiences that would be related to music and just incredible performances. I can think of one a couple of years ago, when Peter and I were in New York and were celebrating my birthday. He asked me what I wanted to do, and there was a place in New York that was in Central Park West where a big band was playing, one of the great big bands. We went to hear that show and the music was so incredible, it was just waving over me and it broke me into tears. It was like there wasn't anyplace I'd rather be or anything else I'd rather be doing.

As far as other things that make me happy, I remember the first time I rode a horse and how I was just grinning ear to ear. I had been reading my horse books for years and years, just dreaming about what it would be like to be on a horse, and there I was. I was riding a horse, and I didn't fall off. I was probably in my teens at the time and being able to actually ride it — just the sense of accomplishment and climbing up on this huge animal — that was great.

I remember the first time I sang in front of a big band and just being happy to be singing and to have seventeen musicians behind me playing on the stage and fifteen hundred people listening — it was such a high . . .

I know what it's like for a performer. It must be a big kick, although I think it's crazy, to perform in stadiums for twenty thousand people. I can imagine what a rush that must be for a performer who's standing there and having like twenty thousand people applaud. I haven't ever had that big an audience, but I know it's got to be an incredible high.

Nancy Currie

Astronaut

Happiest moments? The day my daughter was born. The day I married my husband. Professionally speaking, I'll never forget the day I was selected to become an astronaut, getting that phone call. I literally fell out of my chair. And the calls I've received on all three of my flights to say, you're on this specific mission, start training to go fly in space. I never thought anything could beat, from a professional view, that feeling when I first got told that I was selected to become an astronaut. But when I got told that I was assigned to my first flight, then it was concrete. Then it was, "No kidding, I'm going to go fly in space!" I didn't think I'd ever feel more excited than I did the day I was picked, but I did. So that's something that was very memorable.

Rabbi Stacy Friedman

Rabbi

Anticipating the birth of my baby is really a happy and frightening thing. I've got a month. And getting married was one of my happiest moments. Something about it also was that I spend a lot of time officiating at life-cycle events for other people and because of school and my studies and career, I've postponed a lot of that for myself. So I did it a lot later than some other people. After officiating for other people, being involved for myself and having other people involved is really wonderful.

Valerie Coleman Morris
Anchorwoman/TV personality

I know for me it would be easier to identify my happiest moments at work as opposed to in the fabric and texture of my life. There have been so many happy personal moments, from the birth of children and my oldest being in the delivery room with us when her sister was born to seeing my grandmother in her garden and showing my daughter for the first time how she plants a garden. There are just so many things, right down to my husband and me deciding to get married New Year's Eve afternoon in New York City because Dave Dinkins was going out of office that afternoon and said, "Make an old man happy and let you be my last official act as mayor." That is the most immediate and current personal happy moment.

But to say the happiest in my life—there have been moments, all the way back from when I was a kid, that are happy until someone tells me a reason why they weren't.

This actually happened when I went back for my twentieth high school reunion. Several of the guys I went to school with—and here we were, grown and with children—told me that they really wanted to take me to a dance when I was in high school, but they couldn't because their fathers would have lost their jobs. That's when I realized racism was alive and well when I was there. My parents did this masterful job of making our house the gathering place and fixing up a great basement with a record player so that it was the most appropriate place to have a party. I never realized I wasn't going out on a date, because what was the big deal? I danced with the guys when we'd all hang out together, but when it came down to one-on-one dates, that never really happened. But at the time I thought, "Okay, so I'll have a friend take me." It never became a problem until everybody gave these testimonials. I thought, "My God! That was going on at the time?" [Laughter] But you just realign and kind of go: "Oh."

In fact, I wrote on my *Family Program* about reunions and what it was like. I wrote probably ten pieces about this because it was so revealing. When families come together later in life and things are relived and rethought and realigned, and you learn what the other person was going through or what something really meant, it just gives you new information, and new information gives you new thoughts and hopefully helps you grow.

On the business side, my absolute happiest time in my profession of television was during the heyday of KGO-TV in San Francisco because for me it was journalism in its most absolute and purest form. The years were probably 1974 to 1978. My one daughter was born in 1973 and the other was born in 1977, and so here I was a new mother, with a new job—I had been asked to be a full-time reporter/anchor—so everything was birthing at the same time. I was birthing a daughter, I was birthing a new career. The Oakland/San Jose/San Francisco Bay Area is the place I will always call home because it embraced me in every single way. It's why we will come back home at some point and in some way, near enough to be there regularly, because that is still home for my professional life. I worked with some of the greatest people, and I'm still in touch with them . . . It was just a good time.

I remember distinctly a story of the crash of the KLM jet. It was on a weekend when that happened. We didn't have to make one phone call for anybody to come in and help us on that weekend show. You had camera people showing up, you had people just calling and saying, "I heard this happened. Do you need an extra editor? Do you need this? Do you need that?" It was before companies said you have to get overtime approved or you have to jump through hoops in order to get things done. It was when business and television were really saying it takes cooperative effort to get this on, and let's do it. It was during that same time when there was the tragedy in Jonestown. There was also the Guyana airstrip shooting. That was a weekend story. We were on the air and had to do that. That's the time I remember, and it was wonderful being in the midst of it. It was wonderful having gotten my integrity credentials together at that point, in that time, in that city.

Sylvia Boorstein
Author/Educator/Lecturer

I'm tremendously happy. When I'm working well and teaching well and I know what I know and I get to say it to somebody and get to know that they just got it and I'm a transmitter of that, I'm on fire.

I have had such an abundance of wonderful things in my life. I have six grandchildren, so watching them get born was fantastic. It's amazing. But everything is amazing. I got to get up this morning. We're having this conversation. I can teach. My brain still works.

Reverend Veronica Goines

Presbyterian pastor

I would say that my happiest moments have been times of real connection with people who are significant in my life, such as my kids—just their openness and willingness to trust. There are these times that we've been together that we haven't orchestrated or planned, but just wonderful moments and gifts of time that we've had together.

One of the fondest memories I will carry with me to my grave is the last day that I spent with my mother a few days before she passed. She had cancer, and by the time they discovered [it], it was already metastasized. There was absolutely nothing they could do. We found out about that February 1 and by April 13 she was gone. So it was a very short time, but the greatest joy for me was just spending time with her.

There were times that I would drive across the bay—I'd be working all day—and just sit with her and look at her and touch her for thirty minutes. Then I'd have to go back to work. But this particular day was my off day, and I spent all day with her. I don't think I've ever laughed so much in my life. This woman was so weak and frail, but there was this grace about her. She was just so gracious and loving. I remember the feeling of loving being there with her.

We laughed so much that day, and she was in rare form. Her sense of humor was something else. At the doctor's office we wheeled her in a wheelchair, and she had to get up on the table. So when it was time to leave, we put her back in her chair. We were sitting there in the lobby, and my mom just looked up at my sister and me and said, "Which one of us is going to drive?" We just busted up laughing. That was really special.

It came time for me to begin my trek home, and I couldn't bring myself to leave. I went in to say good night to her because it was going on ten o'clock at night, and I leaned over the bed to kiss her, and she opened her eyes and said, "Bless your heart." It was just so precious.

There have been so many special times. My ordination service in November of 1996 was one, because it seemed like there were people from almost every phase of my life that were there. People traveled to be there, and that meant so much to me. It blew my daughters away. My youngest daughter kept looking around. She said, "Mom, I just can't believe all of these people came." The church was packed. That was very special.

Irene Zisblatt Zeigelstein
Holocaust survivor

People always say to me, "How can you be so happy all the time? Look at your background." I say, "I just love life." I can't forget that I am alive and I make every day meaningful and full because I feel it might be my last.

I do not waste my time with anything negative. It has to be productive, or it has to be positive things. To appreciate life itself—that is a message that many people need.

What I am trying to do in speaking of my past and teaching from my past is to build a hate-free world one student at a time. This is my goal, my aim. Let's say I just speak in a school and I have three hundred students that I'm speaking to. If I can just get one out of that three hundred, that's like having five thousand the next year, because that one person is going to generate that through his or her life. So that is what I am trying to get, one student at a time.

Marti McMahon
Entrepreneur

Some of the happiest moments that I had were the births of my children. I have three children, and I remember all of them being born, being fully wide awake, watching their birth. I had no question in my mind, ever, that I wanted to be a mother, so that fulfillment of actually having my children is very, very special. And now I'm a grandmother, and that was another happy moment. Seeing my boats being christened was an awesome moment for me too, to know that I had actually done that.

I think some of the happiest moments that I have are simply in appreciating each day. I think that that's one of the wonderful things that happens as you grow, that you realize that each day is very precious, and very special.

Jo Hanson
Artist/Environmentalist

I don't think in terms of "happy" or that I can pick out a happy moment. I can pick out moments of satisfaction or great relief. But I don't really think in terms of happiness.

You're probably asking the wrong person. What I aim for is the satisfaction of meaning and of relationships, and that means a lot to me. I love it when there are insights or when you have a wonderful discussion with someone or when the energy flow is really good.

I suppose some people would call that happiness. I don't know. I'm not sure we're designed to be happy. I think we're designed to be meaningful and to take a satisfaction from being meaningful.

If not all of us, I think that's my design. If you were happy all of the time—that's impossible, for one thing. But happiness in that sense would seem to me sort of a stasis.

I can tell you a dramatic moment of satisfaction. It had to do with that cemetery installation I spoke of. That was a terribly complex piece with three major parts, all of them very difficult, and it required enormous problem solving and the development of techniques, logistics, means, and so on.

There was no way to put it all together to install it and see if it worked. Until it was in a museum, I didn't know whether it worked. Its first exhibition was at the Corcoran Gallery in Washington, DC, and I simply was consumed with anxiety.

When it was all up and I saw that it worked, that was one of the greatest reliefs of my life because the preparation and even the job of installing it was so major that if it had been a failure, it would have been a dramatic failure.

It turned out to be really good, and I can still feel the relief of it as I talk about it, the satisfaction of everything working.

But, you know, I can be reading a book and thinking, and get insights about things and make connections, and it's as gratifying to me as something as major as what I just described.

Mary Bitterman

President/CEO, public television

The happiest moments of my life? It's funny, if my husband of thirty-one years were here, he would say, "It takes so little to make her happy."

It's little things that make me happy. I can think of certain stages in my life, or times—they're not really moments. There are times I recall with my parents, especially with my father, whom I was very close to. He died so many years ago that I think there's more of a sense of a loss. I was able to share so much more of my adult life with my mother, who only passed away a couple of years ago. But the various moments that we had together were so joyful.

Times in Hawaii were very special. There was a great moment in Hawaii when my colleagues and I in public broadcasting received the George Foster Peabody Award for this magnificent program we produced on the life of Damian, who was a Belgian missionary to the island of Molokai. People in Hawaii, for various reasons, all of which are ridiculous, have some sense that they are not as good as people on the mainland. It's a sense of second-class citizenship that has people diminish themselves and not feel confident in judging themselves to be really terrific. A lot of what I did at the Hawaii public broadcasting authority was to constantly challenge my good friends and colleagues to raise the bar. So I said I that really thought we should do this story, this wonderful one-man play which was brought to us, and that I would talk to the people at PBS. And the feeling was, "They'll never carry anything from Hawaii." I said, "You know, I just think we have to do this."

And it was really an incredible time. Because when the program was done and we received the greatest national award, the George Foster Peabody Award, it had this sense of ennobling the whole group. That was probably one of the happiest moments in my life, because it was this shared sense of joy and euphoria by everybody. I mean, there were concentric circles. There was the crew who had worked on it. There were all the people who helped fund it. There were all the people who were all the relatives of all the people who had helped fund it and who had been on the crew. There were just plain old Hawaii people who said, "This is so terrific."

I think what made me so happy about it is that once people real-ize they can do really terrific things, and that there's absolutely no excuse for anybody in Hawaii to think themselves less able than some-body who lives in California or Kansas, then that's no longer something that people can rely upon in the future as an explanation or as an excuse. That one's been used up. We can do it; there's no question about it. That made me extremely happy.

There have been very special, happy moments with my wonderful husband and our daughter. But it's sometimes the little things. It's just a sense of good feeling; it doesn't have to be anything huge or fancy. It's a sense of oneness with others, a sense of joy at everybody having worked hard to accomplish something together. It's just the sweetness that sometimes people can show to one another. Those, for me, are really the happiest moments.

Jeanne Rizzo

Entrepreneur

The birth of my son. I think that there's nothing that surpasses that in terms of visceral happiness and totally understanding your womanhood.

I struggled for not that many years. I was married, I was straight and relatively happy in my marriage. I wasn't unhappy in it as a matter of sexuality. But coming to the full appreciation that I'm lesbian and coming out and reconciling that and then being able to fully approach another woman from that place of total acceptance of myself was a very happy moment for me. I'm very happy in my relationship, and I have been for ten years, and I don't have another experience to equate that to. I wake up happy about this relationship every day of my life. It's not a moment; it's a series of moments. I think that having that level of love and that level of commitment inspires me every day. I feel that love repeated, but it comes from a core within myself now that's accepting that I didn't have before. So that's been great for me.

Chapter 8

The Gift of the Spirit

I think flying in space gives you a unique perspective, because I don't see how you could fly in space and not have pretty strong spiritual beliefs. Because when you look out the windows, you don't see this world of chaos. You see this exceptionally beautiful world. Almost indescribably beautiful.

Nancy Currie

The title of this book, Life Messages: Inspiration for the Woman's Spirit, actually evolved after these messages were felt to have a profound effect on the spirit of women—not only the spirit of the reader and author but also the spirit of the very women involved in formulating their thoughts.

Certainly this was true when our conversations turned to spirituality. Spiritual beliefs, religious beliefs, and a belief in a higher philosophy of life have inspired these women in many different ways. Perhaps the majority did not align themselves wholeheartedly with a traditional church, yet each spoke eloquently of the role of the spiritual in their lives. For some, spirituality was a consolation in times of need; for some it was rooted in celebration of good times. Nearly all spoke, in one way or another, of the experience and importance of *connectedness*. Some found this sense of connectedness in God, some in nature, some in an unimaginable yet knowable higher being or purpose. Taken together, their messages are like a prism breaking a single ineffable radiance into a multitude of unique colors.

Isabel Allende
Author

I have no religious beliefs. I cannot take on *any* traditional religion. They're all very patriarchal, all men-oriented, men-controlled. Therefore I cannot call upon those beliefs that I received as a Catholic to help me when I'm down or when I need it. When my daughter was sick I prayed to whatever forces are out there without being able to address the Virgin Mary or God or Christ or whatever because I don't believe in that.

I do believe very strongly in the spirit. We all come from a sort of ocean of spirituality and consciousness. We're all drops of water in that ocean. We need to be in this body to learn something through the senses, through suffering, through joy. Things that only the body can experience. And this feeds, nurtures this ocean with experiences that are important. When I die this particle of spirituality that I am will go back to that common ocean where my daughter is, also. I will not see her in her body, in shape, waiting for me, dressed with a white tunic and wings on the other side. I don't think that will happen at all. I think that she went back to that spiritual form, and I will too. And then maybe we will come back on another planet, in another shape to learn something else. But I don't believe in individual souls. I think that I am made of the same material as you are. Essentially we are identical, you and I and that last tribal man in Papua, New Guinea. The torturer and the saint have essentially the same raw material. Each one of us can potentially be the mass murderer or the saint. If we are able to understand that, we can identify with every single human being.

I also believe that the spirit, this common spirit, is present in everything that exists. In every single animal in nature, in all shapes and forms, in light, in the planets, in everywhere, there is a part that is spiritual. And therefore I have to be extremely respectful of everything that exists because it contains something that is eternal and precious.

Lynn Woolsey

Congresswoman

I don't consider myself a particularly spiritual kind of person because my daughter is and I can see the difference. But I go to church and believe that there's a higher power than human beings, and thank heavens because if we're the highest power then I don't think we're in very good shape. I feel like I do call on that higher power, and I'm not at all embarrassed to shut my eyes and know that something or some spirit outside of me has to be even more in charge of some things than I am in order to make it go right. I have arguments with my children about Christianity and things like that because I believe in God and in Jesus but mostly in a higher spirit.

Carmel Greenwood
Entrepreneur

My father was a lay preacher in Australia. He was quite drunk one day when he was giving the service. He knelt down to give the service and he fell asleep! I'm sitting in the front row, as a child, and he's snoring. My mother was going crazy.

I believe in people having a direct line to God. They don't have to go through a church, and they don't have to go through anyone else.

My daughter is a heroin addict. I was in San Francisco. She'd been in rehabilitation clinics and she was fine for months and months and then something would flip. One day I was so upset I didn't know what to do—she hadn't contacted me. She was on the street in San Francisco. And we're so connected; if she took drugs, *I* felt the repercussions. I couldn't separate. I was going crazy. My whole life was just focused on how I could help her. And I couldn't do anything, I was completely *powerless*. I got down on my hands and knees and asked for help.

The next day a policeman called me from San Francisco and he'd found her. She was very sick. I believe now that it was divine intervention. He was an angel but he was a policeman. And he helped her. He said "If I save one person on the street then my whole career would be worthwhile." It wasn't anything that I said that got her back into rehab. It was what he said. I believe he is an angel.

I think if you believe, you will receive. My beliefs that there are people in the universe to help us have helped me tremendously.

Gretchen Dewitt
Public relations professional

I really changed my concept of God because I think I'd felt that he was a protector. Now I think of God as a comforter and a counselor. And that he's not pulling strings, because he's limited by natural law, and if he were to break natural law, then he would cease to be God, really.

There are, you know, terrible things that happen. You open up a newspaper and there are earthquakes in Afghanistan, tornadoes in South Dakota, and these are laws of the Universe that are eternal with God. So he's not breaking them. We're not protected. I think we can ask for advice and where should we be and what should we be doing. But really, we're in charge of our destinies.

I think religion is different than spirituality. Religion is really a big or small group of people who get together because they share some common beliefs in spiritual matters. So that is what a religion is. I happen to be Mormon. My father was Catholic. And I am a big fan of Catholicism. I believe there is truth and beauty everywhere and that no one has it all. And that all religions have flaws because they are run by people.

Religion is like school. In a way, you go to school because formal education can be very efficient and one learns. But I consider that my spirituality is more important to me than my religion. On the other hand, I probably wouldn't have had my spiritual beliefs without a foundation in a formalized religion.

My beliefs are, I believe in God. I believe in a personal God. I pray to God. That's been an important communication for me, and I have the sense of God enjoying my company. I think he probably likes people checking in with him and telling him they enjoy what they've seen, what they've done. What they have.

I enjoy prayer. I have felt the presence of God in my life. I have felt him. I remember praying, one of the first prayers after my baby died, and I really had a sensation of arms around me. I felt embraced. And I knew—I'm going to weep, of course, for this—but I felt that he was mourning with me, that he was aware of my sadness and was sad because I was sad. I think he rejoices when we rejoice. So I'm a big believer in God. Drama here with the tears.

I believe that life's eternal. I believe that we don't die, that we live forever. I do. I'm a Christian, so it's been easy for me to believe in the Resurrection. When I think about it scientifically it's sometimes hard to grasp. But I think if energy and matter cannot be destroyed, and all energy and matter take on new forms, then it makes sense that it would be impossible to destroy the spirit. And perhaps the spirit is the mind of man that is separate from the brain, which is a muscle that we are born with. With this individual spirit that we have, we have encoded information and I believe that that's why really all civilizations from the beginning of time have believed in a god—not because it gave them power, saying "I know what causes the rain or the lightning," not because it would make them know more, or it would give them control—I think because we have a knowledge of God in us.

And I'm partly agnostic because I believe in that divine spark, that we have that information, we have all kinds of information. I think it's there in us, so we are aware of God. That part of God is in us. Information of all kinds is encoded in our minds, and it's up to us to decode. That's why televisions are invented, and airplanes and nuclear submarines and cures for cancer. We come to Earth as astronauts with information. It's sort of a reverse of going to the moon, that we're coming from the spiritual world to this world with information. We don't come here with nothing. And so we have this knowledge of God and we have information stored, and we have the computer inside us and we have to learn how to work the computer.

So I thought of the astronauts as they went off. I did a reverse sort of "Imagine little babies coming here." Maybe in another existence in the spiritual world we were told there was a beautiful place out in space and that there would be risks to take, but we would have bodies. As we existed then in a preexistence, premortality, we didn't have bodies. And with bodies we could paint, and climb mountains and make love, and do things we couldn't do. Were we willing to come here and take risks with these bodies? And probably we thought this was a good idea. We would come and take these risks.

Alice Waters
Restaurateur/Author/Educator

I don't have any real religious beliefs. Mother Nature.

I mean, I think there's something enormous to be understood about nature . . . I get overwhelmed and awed by the beauty, the complexity . . . the healing power, I guess you might say.

I love having my garden, even if I don't get a chance to tend it like I want, still it's very important to me. I like just going out and picking things in it and being able to be that connected with the food that's grown. There's something amazing about that.

Leslie Young
Ballet soloist

I have my Christian faith. I grew up in a Presbyterian Church, and now I'm a member of Grace Cathedral, which is Episcopal, so it's always been in the Protestant side of religion. I believe in God. I do believe that all of these wonderful moments in my life have been blessings from him.

Prayer is a very big thing that I fall upon when I'm anxious. I am supported by a good support system with my family and my husband, and my husband's family. They all have the same foundation in Christianity. That is very good for support and communication.

Yes, I think it's very comforting to be able to talk to God about my anxiety, and to be asking for help. Also to have someone to be thankful to, to say thank you for all these wonderful things. There are times when I think your soul needs to express emotions, whether in praise or fear or sadness . . . Dancing is a way of expressing my soul in a physical sense, and I think prayer is this other sense.

I know I don't always ask for the right things, but that's all part of it as well. I can be thankful for things that have happened that aren't exactly what I asked for. But in my faith I know that this is what is best for me, that I have a loving God who is giving me what is best for me and it isn't necessarily something that I'm going to understand exactly at that moment. And I may never understand in my life. But that's okay with me because that's what I trust in; that's what I believe in.

Annelies Atchley
Educator/Artist

At some point during childhood the spirit is born and then the spirit comes into the body and from that point that spirit grows and grows and grows and grows and grows, and when you die and your body is gone, you're out spiritually. Our body is born to bear a spirit. I don't think we're born as babies with a spirit. I think the spirit comes into us at about six, seven, eight. You see kids go religious at that time. They suddenly have a spirit about God and you see that. I think when you're born you're like a liver or heart. If you take a liver out of a person, it dies. I really think we're born as an organ and then nurturing and caring will make our bodies grow and in that nurturing and caring body there is a spirit born.

I've been teaching kindergarten and I know that there is a little person and suddenly there is a spirit born and sometimes I think, "Ooh, look." One child asks another in kindergarten—I heard this one day—"Do you believe in God?" This one girl says, "Yes." And she says, "God is just like the air around us." That's a very spiritual thing for a little child to say. I'm sure she heard some of it but part of it is there's this little spirit born into that.

I don't believe children are born with a spirit right out of the body of the mother because we're an organ then. That's how my political beliefs are too. I believe in abortion and the choice of the woman because I think I'm totally pro-family but I'm also pro-child because I think every child should be wanted. I think that if two cells meet, that's not a spirit and that's not a child and that's not a body. It's an organ. What we do with that organ is our responsibility.

I tragically had an abortion. I don't regret it because I wouldn't have wanted that child to come into the world I had at the time. It's still a very sad, sad thing I'll always carry around, but I know I did a good thing because that little spirit that wanted to come into that baby of mine is now in another body and has a better family than what I could give it then.

Laurel Burch

Artist

I *have a sense of life and the mystique* of it; the things that I don't understand are the things that I don't understand,

and the preciousness of it all is something that I am aware of all the time. As far as higher beliefs—these are harder things for me to talk about . . .

Usually the term "faith" is a companion to religion. You usually hear that word in context with church or organized thing, religion, and I don't mean it that way at all. But in a very real and true sense of what that word means, I have that . . . knowing that your heart can be broken, that you can recover, and that your spirit can be broken, and that you can experience something on the other side of that . . . Even though different challenges look different each time, the healing spirit and the life spirit is so capable of growing and renewing and evolving and healing and enrichening. And a lot of my beliefs are based on the awareness of that. A way that it's helped me is I think it gives me, personally, at a really intimate level, things like my courage, my passion.

I keep using the word "richness," and that's the word I think of. It's a kind of richness, the dynamic.

A lot of my beliefs kind of transformed in the last few years. As I grew up, I had deep, deep connectedness with people, but in terms of all of life as a whole, I feel much more humbled by what I've seen and experienced personally in the last several years and I feel more aware of a kind of partnership. It's hard to explain, but it feels like a partnership. I'm much more totally aware of a common thread between all living things. I felt it before, but not the same way I have in the last few years. And that feeling and that awareness is helpful in terms of being at peace with one's self. That's the value that I see in it. It's feeling a connectedness and a kind of peacefulness as a result, a belonging.

Sue Backman

Entrepreneur/Billiards professional

I went through the usual question of not just political authority but religious authority when I was in my late teens. I did a lot of reading of comparative literatures. I went through a fascination with Judaism. At this point I call myself an Episcopalian Buddhist. It covers a lot of bases.

I don't particularly belong to a particular church but especially in the last couple of years, I have gotten back into a lot more reading and I would say probably half of the stuff I read is on religion, spirituality, and those kinds of things. Then a couple of years ago a very interesting thing happened that was a big life changer for me and that was that a very good friend of mine is a Reiki master. Basically it is a way of channeling energy for relaxation and healing. Many people are familiar with the concept of Chi from that and it's really very similar, but the main difference with Reiki is that it is purely for healing and relaxation. It's not used for anything else, like in Chinese Chi work, where you can sometimes use it for defense and all kinds of things. This is purely for the healing, and when you get the attunement, you become a protected channel. What that means is that if you're working with someone who has physical or mental or emotional problems that you're hopefully running energy through to balance and cure, it can't come back to you. With other Chi work, that's a danger. It can deplete you. But with Reiki that can never happen. It's a one-way channel that goes through you to that person. It can never come back and harm you in any way. As you are the channel, you receive the benefit of that energy as it comes through you to the other person. So you're giving yourself a Reiki treatment at the same time.

Of course I can give myself a Reiki treatment just by putting my hands on myself, and I'm doing that more and more now, but initially I did it with the idea of being able to help other people. Not so much myself. So that was a big thing for me, and I think that was what started a whole series of shifts in me mentally and emotionally. The following year, when I received a second attunement, there was a huge energy shift in me. What happens with each attunement is you're able to handle higher and higher levels of energy. Many times more with each one. After the second one I noticed that all of a sudden my ability to try and hold down my emotions had shifted greatly and instead of keeping things in and keeping my mask on and being very controlled about my emotions, I was becoming much more reactive. If I felt something, I would say it. If I was angry, I would tell somebody and I wouldn't hold it. I used to be famous for just holding something in until I exploded. I didn't do that anymore. At first it was scary for me. But then I realized it was really a gift and I felt like I was much more in control and much more effective in some ways. I think other people during that period of time thought, "Gee. What's going on with Sue? She didn't used to act like that." I think they're starting to get used to it now, hopefully. But I'm not afraid to show my emotions anymore, and I think that's a good thing.

Nancy Currie

Astronaut

Because of the nature of what we do, there are certain phases, particularly during ascent, when your options are somewhat limited if things start to go very wrong. You literally have to come to grips at some point with the fact that you're in God's hands and you're relying on him to keep you safe.

I think flying in space gives you a unique perspective, because I don't see how you could fly in space and not have pretty strong spiritual beliefs. Because when you look out the windows, you don't see this world of chaos. You see this exceptionally beautiful world. Almost indescribably beautiful. But it's also a world of great order. It's not chaotic, it's very orderly. There's a lot of symmetry. So you really have the sense that a higher being did this and was responsible for all of this. And it's a real lesson, and it teaches you to be very humble, I think, once you've flown in space and seen this universal perspective. Because what's driven home and the overriding thing that you feel is how small in the world your place really is. You just feel exceptionally small, and you hope that in this vast universe you can make just a hint of a difference, because the enormity of it is somewhat overwhelming.

When we designed our last patch, we put a rainbow on it. In the book of Genesis, Chapter 9, it talks about how the sign of God's covenant with all his people is when the rainbow appears in the sky. In the NASA official write-up of the patch, you'll see no reference to it.

Well, we were launching at night, and when we woke up in the afternoon, it was raining at the Cape. So we initially thought, "Oh boy, we're going to have a hard time launching tonight, you can't launch in the rain." And a short time later, the rain stopped and over the shuttle this incredible rainbow appeared. In fact, a few folks took a picture of it and sent it to us.

On the fourth day of the flight, our families pick wake-up music. Normally that's selected about a month ahead of time, and they say, "What songs would you like us to play to wake up the crew that maybe have special meaning?" Well, the commander's daughter had chosen about a month ahead of time the song "Somewhere Over the Rainbow." So we thought that was just a little bit too much coincidence. Because everything did go so well.

We really felt blessed during the mission, and we talked about that several times. Also I flew a Bible, and several other crew members flew their favorite Scripture readings, and we shared them in orbit. It's a really unique place and a really unique perspective, you know, as you're flying over the South Pacific in a lightning storm, to share those sorts of things.

Rabbi Stacy Friedman
Rabbi

For me, a spiritual tradition on its own out by myself somewhere would feel empty; it wouldn't be complete. So for me a spiritual life in the context of a community—whatever religion that is—is so important and I think that it's a way also to not be so self-absorbed.

There's a lot of sadness and emptiness because people are so self-absorbed. I remember when I was a freshman in college and really having a hard time and what saved me was this little sign. I went to Brandeis, which was a Jewish university, and there was a little sign that said: "Do you want to feel happy? Call this number for Project Ezra." In Hebrew the word "Ezra" means help. I thought, "I want to feel happy," so I called that number and said, "What is this Project Ezra?" They said, "Every Saturday we go to nursing homes and do services." So I started doing that, and it saved me because I started feeling happy. I started giving back, and that's a religious thing. It's also spiritual. So I think becoming part of the community and helping each other again and becoming big families is one of my favorite things about being part of a religious community. We have 1,100 families here, and people help each other. I just think it would be so lonely not to be part of that.

Sometimes if I just visit people in the hospital, they say, "Thank you so much." And I say, "Thank you for allowing me to do that, because it feels so good to be able to do that . . ."

One more thing about belief in a higher good. We also believe in the Jewish tradition—and it's a real central belief and I think one that's important—that when we were each created, we were created with two inclinations, the inclination for good and the inclination for evil. We were not created perfectly good or evil or anything like that but with an inclination for good and evil, and our job in life is obviously to make the good come out over the evil. Sometimes we get too much in the evil and can ask for forgiveness and straighten ourselves out. So I think that both good and evil are inherent in our world and that our job is just to try to make the good win out over the evil. I don't think it's God's fault when evil or bad things happen, although I try to remember and praise God when good things happen and not necessarily to blame when bad things happen.

It's our job to make the world a better place. There's this spiritual notion in Judaism, this mystical notion, that when God created the world it was so blindingly bright that there was a vessel that encapsulated God and God blew up the vessel and there are pieces of it all over the world. Those are the little pieces of God all over. So it's our job to try to repair this vessel that contains God's glory and that's too bright to look at and there are little pieces of it. You know, when you help somebody across the street or give somebody a dollar or don't yell at somebody or whatever it might be . . .

Valerie Coleman Morris
Anchorwoman/TV personality

I always say to people, whether it is your god or the universe or whatever the higher power is, there has to be one, and I think it's very important that we vocalize whatever that is. For some people it's nature. Just communing with nature is a spiritual experience. Whatever it is, I do believe that spirituality is critically important.

I think we all call upon our beliefs in times of need. What I try to do is always call upon my beliefs when everything is going *well*. I have a book that I read every day. It's called *Acts of Faith for People of Color*, and it's just a one-page thought for every day, and I read it every single day. I think the instinct is you pray or you ask for assistance and you make promises when you're in need but when things are going well, we aren't as deliberate in that communication with whatever a higher being is. So I try and make sure that I do it on a regular basis so I'm not just asking.

A lot of that spirituality was originally from Mud—my grand-mother—but I'm very grateful, and I don't use that word very often, but I guess I'm very grateful to my youngest daughter, who has embodied the spirituality of her great-grandmother and has been that way since being a very small child. She's the person who can just embrace my spirit and kind of soothe it. It's always very interesting because she knows that my favorite word is reciprocity and she'll say, "Who taught you that?" She does something for me and I say, "Thank you so much. I just really needed to be a little clearer on that." And she'll say, "But who taught me?" So I think that's a great gift.

Spirituality is very important and I try to address that when I talk to everybody but especially young people. Just reminding them that God, Allah, whatever name he is, doesn't judge according to your body or your appearance. There's an expression in Islam that says—I'm paraphrasing here—Allah doesn't judge according to your body's appearances, but he scans your hearts and looks into your deeds. I think that applies to us.

Sylvia Boorstein
Author/Educator/Lecturer

"Believe" is such a potent word for people. What I find is that I try not to answer the question of "This is what I believe." Because what I like to say is, "This is what out of my experience I have

come to trust. I trust that when I am paying attention and when I am telling myself the truth, I can manage my life and do more than that. I can hold it, I can be grateful within it, I can relate to it with compassion, I can relate to other people with compassion. I cannot be in an adversarial stance with my life and with my experiences with other people. I do not have to feel separate. I can feel connected. I don't have to be pleased with what's going on in order to be content."

That is the major discovery of my whole spiritual life: You don't have to like what's happening in order to be happy or be content. I can't always do it, but I trust that it is possible to move the vision of one's mind and heart from the smallness of the immediate drama, from *my* life, to life itself, and life itself is always remarkable and awesome. Sometimes I get stuck and I can't move into that place. When I can't, I know that I can't and I hope I am compassionate with myself rather than being mad at myself.

Sometimes in the past I have thought that if I were really a spiritual person I would be able to be in that place all of the time. That passed away. It's a complicating story. We tell ourselves complicated stories all of the time to make our lives worse. "If I were really spiritual, anger would never arise." "If I were really spiritual, I would never get depressed." "If I were really spiritual, I could feel God's glory in every moment." That's not true. If I'm too tired, if I'm too overwhelmed, if I'm too frightened, if one of my children's health is imperiled, I get frightened. I get frightened and my mind closes in. My drama becomes of preeminent importance. It is not *the* drama, it is *my* drama, and I suffer and I'm in pain like everybody else.

I trust that another stance is a possibility. That's what I trust, the potential of the human mind and heart, and my prayer life is enormously important in reestablishing a wider mind space so that I can know that.

Reverend Veronica Goines
Presbyterian pastor

There was a scripture that I read early on in my life and it really came to have much more meaning for me in relationship to my ministry, and that verse says that a person's gifts make room for them in this world and take them before great people. In other words, we sometimes end up in places or situations that we don't envision because we can't see that big. That certainly was something I just took to heart. I remember when I read it and something within me said, "Yes." I knew it was true and I tucked it away.

When I was finishing up seminary, my pastor said to me, "Veronica, a person's gifts make room for them." At that time I was really stressing over where I was going to end up and what ministry I would be in. So there was this sense of being reminded. When he said that it just bubbled back up again. I said, "Yes, I knew that." But it was so wonderful for him to remind me. I was again at peace and not worried about what was going to happen.

I had already applied for the pastorate here at St. Andrew, but it took a long time before I heard anything because I caused quite a ripple in the system being a person who was not a Presbyterian applying for a Presbyterian pastorate. So all the committees didn't know what to do with me. The church was saying, "Listen. We've looked at over a hundred dossiers. We know this is the person God is sending to us." They said, "Yeah, right." And yet once people would meet me face-to-face and we'd have an opportunity to talk, I could just see their shoulders going down and they would just kind of relax.

Irene Zisblatt Zeigelstein
Holocaust survivor

. . . And that was the first day, the first experience that I had in the camp, and I could not understand why I was there and why we were all there. We had no windows in the barrack, but we had a little opening between the roof and the wall and I couldn't breathe, I guess it was anxiety, and I stuck my mouth out there to get some fresh air and then I heard some screams coming from the distance and they were getting closer and closer, and then I saw a convoy of trucks passing on the road and two children, like the age of maybe two, three years old. They fell out of the truck and the truck stopped and the SS man from the truck came out and the children were screaming, and he picked up these children and he hit them against the truck. Of course they stopped screaming, and I saw this blood running down the truck and I, I just, I just can never forget that. And I looked up to heaven, and I said to God, "Why are you letting the children die such a cruel death? They have not even thought about living and they are already dead." And of course he didn't answer me, and I thought, "Well the Germans took God and they killed God so they can do this to our children." And

I got numb, like I had no feeling in my body, and I must have fallen asleep.

When I got up in the morning, I thought about what I saw the night before. I was trying to get up, focus on it, to see whether it was a dream, or an illusion, or the real thing. But it was the real thing because the girl next to me said, "We heard those screams last night too, but what did you see?" And I said, "Where is God?" and they said, "He's everywhere." And I said, "Well, he's not here." But the next day in my thirteen-year-old mind, I thought, "The Germans killed him." But I was no longer thirteen years old because I was already a thirteen-year-old adult, and I just figured it out that maybe God is somewhere where he is needed more than he is needed here and when he finishes his job he will come and help us. And so I decided "I will not burden him with my problems and I'll never ask him to help me or anybody else," and I didn't the whole time I was in camp. I never asked him for help, for myself or for anybody else.

Marti McMahon
Entrepreneur

I have been blessed with a tremendous faith. I was brought up as a Catholic, and I do believe in a spiritual being. I do believe in God. To me, it is God. And I pray a lot. That doesn't necessarily mean getting on your hands and knees all the time and praying. It just means when you're driving around in a car, it could be just thanking God for what you have and also asking the higher being to guide you, what your next step should be.

When I was getting divorced, my mother was also dying of cancer and it was such a low point in my life at that point, and without my faith, I think I would have just lost it. And I think also during that time too I did question my father because I knew that my mother, who was extremely religious and brought me up blessing me every time I left the door, was suffering so greatly I just couldn't understand that and that was extremely difficult for me. But I also believe that people that pass on are still with you. And I pray to my mother all the time, and whether you could call it praying or speaking to, she still is a very big part of my life and she's been gone for fifteen years. And yet she isn't. She's still there. And there are people that I know that have special powers . . . When I was in high school, there was a nun. She was my mentor then and she passed away after my mother did, but she used to pray for me every day in her prayer book for as long as she knew me. And I know that she also is looking out after me somewhere and looking out after my children. I absolutely do believe in that.

Jo Hanson

Artist/Environmentalist

I am strongly spiritual. I think that's a dominating thing of my life, but they're not religious beliefs. I do find the mythologies of all the religions interesting and I like reading and understanding. But spirituality for me is more a thing of natural process and a growing awareness of the way everything is connected. The nature of the universe as a web of energy. English is a wonderful language, but it doesn't have a vocabulary for spiritual discussion. It gets difficult. As you live you observe that you do one thing here and it affects something here and it affects something there and there, and you see that as part of your experience . . .

What you see in natural process is that indeed everything is connected, everything is energy, that the energy takes form in patterns and that all patterns are interrelated until you get to cosmic scale . . . Energy doesn't have a break in it or exist in isolated pockets. It's impossible. Because energy is movement. Energy is change. You can't have an isolation of energy. You can have a blockage that comes out some other way . . .

The idea of existence being mechanical and material just can't be supported by what you see and know or what you live. This is particularly true, I think, when you live close to nature. I was always terribly urban. It never occurred to me that I would do something bizarre like getting a place at the Russian River and spending as much time as I could up there. Being close to nature is so constructive. You see the intelligence of the system, and there's nothing automatic about an ecosystem. An ecosystem is a living energy system that is constantly monitoring itself and regulating itself. If you need more redwood soil, that's the chemistry in this system. If the bays are getting overactive, the chemistry tones them down a little. My point is that they're living, intelligent systems and you see the intelligence and the way aggressive plants will slip in under cover of big leaf plants and the way things that you don't want will intertwine themselves in the roots of the things that you do want. They give you an ultimatum: It's both of us or neither. This is all very instructive and you just can't deny it when you see it and know it. That's the nature of my spirituality.

I learned that all change is creation. There's change that we don't like, and we call that destruction. There's change that we like, and we call that creation. But it's all creation.

The flood was creating a new situation then. As I became more knowledgeable, I understood the flood was creating diversity, habitat, fresh soil . . . it was soaking the roots of the trees and doing very valuable things.

That's why you see in nature that every waterway has a flood bank. When you hear a flood called a "natural disaster," you have to keep in mind that that's not quite right. It's a natural event that's very important to be happening. I guess the disaster would be people who get in the flood plain or build houses in the flood plain.

The processes are continuous. There's never an end . . .

Infinity stopped being a mind thing and became a body thing. I knew about infinity. It still blows my mind that within the past year I saw a photo of stars and the celestial system taken with a camera located on a satellite that allowed photography that was never possible before. What it was showing was the explosion of stars and birth of new stars, which is exactly the same thing. There is a continuous process of the explosion and renewal, and it's a continuous process of creation that has no beginning and no end.

I still don't quite understand that, but I know in my tissues that it happens. The reason is that it's energy and energy has to change. That's the nature of energy.

Mary Bitterman

President/CEO, public television

Spiritual beliefs, religious beliefs . . . I certainly have a sense of values, those values by which I guide my behavior and which are, I'm certain, more important to me than they are to others. Except as people, this sounds odd, may benefit from my practice of my values. For example, I believe it's very important to be honest, to be responsible, to be reliable, to have my word be my bond. To be compassionate, to extend oneself, to appreciate the suffering or the difficulties that others are experiencing, and to try to bring something of a remedial nature, however modest, to that situation. A value of treating all people with dignity.

Even though I was raised in one religious tradition, the Roman Catholic tradition, my life has been spent in ways that have been so greatly enriched by very close friends and colleagues who are Jewish and Buddhist, in large part, that I don't have a sense that there is only one religious outlook that has value. I think that those things that world religions in most part share is the notion of extending respect to others and leading an honorable life. And those are the things that are important to me.

I think in general it's important to have a moral compass. Sometimes people will say, "Why do you have to be honest if the people you're dealing with are dishonest? Why do you not shriek obscenities at people who are outrageous in their conduct with you?" In a way my answer has always been that I have to be myself. I don't have power over a lot of things. I have some power to influence—every human being does. And with the nature of my work and the fact that I am engaged in a larger community, there is some possibility for making a difference. And I feel very responsible, that any influence I would exert would be for the public good. But it's very important to me that I have, that I retain the power to be myself. I don't want to engage in vulgarities. I don't want to be a cruel or rude person. I have no interest in that. I don't think it is any demonstration of lack of strength or whatever, not to lower oneself to a lifestyle that you really feel uncomfortable with. I feel sad sometimes that in our society there's the notion that the people who scream and yell are somehow very strong. I think it shows a lack of self-control, I think it shows a kind of buzzing, blooming confusion.

I've always been much more attracted to the reflective, to the more quiet show of strength. I have not seen any example of a person demonstrating strength to me by diminishing others. I have oftentimes felt quite sorry for people who behave in a manner that is out of control and not attractive, and most of the time I think just sort of pathetic. The people who are intolerant and call up hatred toward others, they are just not the people that I would look to to provide an example to anyone.

I think my belief in the equality of people, in the dignity of people, and in living a life that is a good, "ethical" life, is really at the core of my being. And I can't veer from those positions. Those are kind of at the heart of it.

Sister Mary Neill

Nun/Author/Educator

I remember when my mother was dying, it was very hard to sustain because she just wouldn't die. And she tried and she wouldn't. And then I was in therapy and the therapist broke the container, he abandoned me. My spiritual director abandoned me. Honest to God, I was in the pit of all pits. I'd say to my friends, "Do you believe in anything?" They'd say yes, and I'd say, "Well I'm going to borrow your faith. I have none." They'd say, "Do you love anything?" I would say yes, and they'd say, "Well, I'm going to borrow it," and I would say, "Do you have faith, hope, and love?" So these enterprises that we undertake with this profound hubris, a pride as if we're here to place faith, hope, and love in the world are undertaken only with others' hands.

One of the telling stories of my life concerns the time when I was returning from Europe. I was wearing my habit at the time—in France I had worn my habit at first but I got a snit on, and I thought "I can't do this," so I didn't wear it but on going home I was wearing it—and this guy said, "Are you a real nun?" And he said, "Well, I'm an atheist." I said, "A real atheist? All I ever met was someone trying to get their mother off their back and hurt her by saying they don't believe in God."

So for twelve hours we sat on a plane together and we just talked and talked and talked. I said that being a theologian in study, more and more I knew I had a part that didn't believe in God, that being a theologian led you to disbelief because this isn't God, this isn't God, this isn't God, so what is God? So that now I knew that my atheist kept me clean. That part of me that wanted to give over my soul, in some kind of emergent way, was kept clean by my atheist saying "Mary, that's not God. Who says this is God?"

And so I said, "What does an atheist do with the part that believes?" He said, "When my mother died I wanted to believe. I wanted to believe that I would see her again."

So we talked for long hours, he about him and IBM, how he made it through the system, and I about the church and how I made it through the system. And as he's getting off the plane, he says to me, "Sister, I worry about you." He gave me his card. He said, "I never met a nun like you." I said, "I didn't either." "So how will you make it in the system?" I mean he could see that I was going to have a terrific culture shock, coming home to reinstate myself into religious life, and he was right. He had more sense of how systems work and what they did with mavericks than I did. So he said, "I never met a nun like you." And I said, "I never did either."

I think that is the issue for every role I met. I never met a mother like you, I never met you, who are you, I never met a writer like you . . . The peculiarity, the individuation, to me that is what Christ represents, that the individual carries God in a very unique way. That where we remain in God is an absolute unique place. And no one is going to understand it. Really. And you're not going to understand it. There are people who can cheer it on.

So years later the card fell out and I thought, "Maybe I'll call this guy." Then I thought, "No, that's a perfect gift. This was a gift, complete in itself." And again, affirmation from strangers . . .

I'm not hung up on the word "God" because I know for many people, it's hurtful to them, but if you are on the right path, the structures will both hold you and fight you. And you will grow strong in struggling with those structures. I can see that the kids sitting in front of me, they haven't had the structures. They don't have a Pope they can hate. They don't have a mother and father that's on their back. What are they going to struggle with in order to become strong? So to be a Catholic is to honor forms and know that those forms are necessary . . . It's like you have to struggle with the forms and then you have to pull it where there is no form. This again is where Buddhism is very helpful. Many of the great theologians who studied in the East, like Thomas Merton, Donatello, Johnson, felt that all Roman Catholics ought to take Buddhist practice because it's the negative imprint of Catholicism. Catholicism is full of mystery and incense and forms. Buddhism is the zipped down religion. It really questions. It has a form, but it really looks at the nothingness under the forms. So that's been very, very helpful to me.

Jeanne Rizzo

Entrepreneur

I'm definitely not religious. We can go there right away. It's more a matter for me of understanding that I'm here in this body on this planet in this moment and I carry a soul to this body and I'm here as a gift and that all around me I feel the air and the earth and the mountains and everything that's living I feel like I share on this planet. So I feel a camaraderie with the planet and I feel I'm at one with that when I'm caretaking, when I'm being respectful of that.

My spirituality, if anything, has a Buddhist sense. That would be my goal and my striving would be when I can meditate to that place. When I can really feel my oneness with the planet. When I'm sitting on top of Ring Mountain and I can find a peaceful place because the challenge for me is to disengage from all of the worldly things and feel myself in that centered place and to meditate to that place. When I'm there and when I'm at one, I feel that I come from a place of compassion, a place where I suspend judgment, a place where I can feel true love for everything that comes in front of me. Then I can find the love place in every person that I meet and I can feel compassion. So that's my challenge. That's my work. To let go of judgment and find compassion . . . I feel that I have an ongoing need and responsibility to do that and then I will do that work from that place and I will fulfill my destiny, which is to make a difference on the planet and to model that to my son. I would like to leave this earth and have my son hold that model and say, "My mom was on this earth; she made a difference and I loved her for that." Then I'll feel that I fulfilled my spiritual obligation.

Chapter 9

The Magic of Intuition

I have a lot of confidence in intuition. It's the one thing you

have to have in art, because art is guided a lot by intuition.

It's intuition that tells you when something works and when

it doesn't. It suggests to you ways to deal with it and tells you

when to stop.

Jo Hanson

Intuition is a sometimes maligned concept that can
evoke an antiquated image of women. Yet the accomplished women in
this chapter readily acknowledge that they place a great deal of confidence in their individual sense of intuition, whether they think of it as
an inner voice, as the distillation of unconscious learning, or as divine
guidance. Although they differ in their experience of intuition, all
agree that it is a reality that enhances our ability to direct our lives.

Isabel Allende

Author

Naturally, I believe in intuition. This is what my life is about: impulse! About doing things without thinking, just because they should be done!

I think that intuition is information that we have gathered in an unconscious way. Often, for example, I'm in a restaurant and I'm paying attention to what my husband is saying and, to a certain extent, the food. But I'm also, without being aware, paying attention to other conversations at other tables. I get little pieces of information here and there. I'm aware of the body language of the waiter. I'm aware of the space. I'm not, of course, conscious that this is information I am gathering. Yet it's all stored inside me in a place that is very deep. I reach that place sometimes in dreams, and I retrieve information that I don't know I have.

Why is it that sometimes I enter into a room, let's say a cocktail party, and I just can't stay? I have to leave because I feel very uncomfortable. I leave because my intuition says, "This is not good for you. People are smoking, this is small talk, you're not interested, you're wasting your time, your feet are hurting. Why are you here? This is a waste of time." My intuition is telling me that, and I'm not listening. Now I do listen, and if I feel uncomfortable, I leave. Because I know that I have enough experience in my life, enough information to know that this is not good for me.

I also have some strange intuition about babies. I know when someone in my family is pregnant before they do. I know if the baby is going to be a boy or a girl. If I have dreams, the child comes with a name. That's how I named my kids. I saw all my grandchildren after they were conceived, but before the mother even knew she was pregnant.

Lynn Woolsey
Congresswoman

I believe in intuition a great amount. I tease myself and others about me being a witch. I can give so many examples, but here is one good example. I said, "It's been years since I heard of so and so." And that night at the movie, so and so sat right in front of me. It happens over and over. I can be thinking of somebody, and they will be in my life within a very short time frame.

It's taken my congressional and campaign staff a long time to be able to say—and now they know it and understand it and mean it— "Listen to Lynn. Her gut is never wrong." It's really a mistake if I overlook what my gut is telling me. It's like, "Come on, you guys. I tell you this isn't the right thing to do because I feel sick inside about it." Or "I know it's the right thing to do." I have had to be able to learn how to verbalize a lot of my passion, which I didn't used to do. It's very important.

Carmel Greenwood

Entrepreneur

I believe in intuition one hundred percent. I learned my lesson in my financial business, because a week before the crash came I heard a voice in my ear saying, "Sell." I phoned up all the brokers in town, and they said, "No, no, no. The market will go up at least another twenty percent." I said, "Okay, you guys know more than me. I didn't even go to high school." So I didn't sell. The day before the crash came, this voice again said, "*Sell!*" So I went to the office and sold all the stock for all my clients. I spoke to my husband, who said, "No, no, no." We didn't sell ours until the next day, and we lost some money. So I learned to trust my intuition.

If I hadn't trusted my intuition with my son, Christopher, who was in Sydney while I was in Hong Kong, I wouldn't have known that he was in trouble with drugs, because he had sworn his sister to secrecy. And I wouldn't have been able to help him.

I'm guided. I know I'm divinely guided in my path. And now I follow it one hundred percent. If I'm told to heal someone, I might phone them up and say, "I'm told to give you a healing." Sometimes they'll hang up on me, but six months later they'll come!

I'm told to tell people certain things; people think I'm crazy. And I think, "Horrors, you ask me to do this?" But now I just do it. I'll follow my intuition. I may not have logical explanations. I'll pick up and go somewhere at the drop of a hat, or I will be going on a trip and I'll cancel it. I follow my intuition.

Gretchen Dewitt
Public relations professional

My mother told me when I was young that my gut instinct would be correct ninety percent of the time. So I'm a big believer in intuition. I think that when we rethink things, we murk up the waters, we make things muddier. I think that we have very good intuition, though some have better intuition than others.

It's like how the rabbit in the forest knows intuitively that the owl could be a problem. We have those intuitions about people and situations, and we need to listen very carefully and not intellectualize too much, because our intuitions are really telling us what is out there. They are seldom wrong. I can remember so many times of disregarding an intuition about someone, when really my gut reaction to that situation, to that person, was correct.

Intuition is part of our very earliest beginnings. It's a part of us that is not insignificant. I think it's crucial.

Alice Waters
Restaurateur/Author/Educator

Yes, I believe in intuition, probably too much. But I feel like I listen very carefully to it. I'm looking for that voice to tell me. And just getting a sense. I think that happens a lot more when your senses are fine-tuned and you can pick up on it. But I do believe in it.

Rosie Casals
Professional athlete

I think I'm very intuitive. I think I can grasp things and feelings and say, "Oh, I think I need to go in that direction" or "I don't think this is right for me. I think we need to think about it." Those are intuitions that you get, and you learn to trust them. If they are important and you follow them, and you've been successful in having the right results, then you continue.

Leslie Young
Ballet soloist

Yes, I believe in intuition. Where it comes from I'm not exactly sure. And I don't always trust my intuition, I guess. I wish I would, because there are always those moments when I think, "See! I knew it!"

One day I was walking through Safeway, and I had this revelation. All of sudden I stopped and looked around, and people were not people, but they were souls walking around. It made me think about how I really believe that our physical bodies are just shells, and here are all these souls walking around. The souls looked nothing like the bodies that they were encased in, and I looked around thinking, "This may be the only time I see you and you and you and you." And I just had this moment of enjoying creation and realizing how many people there are and they all have their lives, and I have my life. I thought, "Here we are, in this community at Safeway, sharing this place and this moment. And they're all going to go off, and I don't know anything about their lives. I don't know anything." But I was appreciating their lives at that moment, and I was very grateful that they were here on this earth. It was this funny revelation moment, this little vision that I think still goes with me when I go shopping. When I'm driving along, passing people in cars, I look at them and think how we are all here on this earth at the same time together. Maybe I'll talk to them, maybe I won't. Maybe our lives will intersect, maybe they won't. You let someone go ahead of you in line because they have one item and you have twelve. And just that little smile and thank-you, you never know. You never know.

Breaking boundaries. There aren't the boundaries that society has created. In the revelation at Safeway, there were no boundaries. Everyone had a soul. And that's true whether you're in this high executive office suite or if you're a janitor somewhere. I'm not saying that those are extremes, but just that you still have a soul, and that they weigh the same to me.

Annelies Atchley
Artist/Educator

All my life I've been intuitive. You can call it faith or intuition. For me, I didn't think God was looking over me, because I thought God was punishing me. So I had to just do it intuitively.

I think I'm a kindergarten teacher because I read the children's eyes and read their spirit. I intuitively read animals that I love, I read nature, I read ecology, I read people. Then I feel intuitively what they need and want and what I have to do.

I think women are especially intuitive. Everyone is, but women are even more.

Sue Backman

Entrepreneur/Billiards professional

Do I believe in intuition? Absolutely. And I place a lot of confidence in it. The more I use it, the more confident I am. I think the only thing I regret is times when I have had the little whispering in the ear and I've ignored it: "Gee, I should have. I *knew* I should have." Those kinds of things.

I'm getting better at it now, at going "Pay attention." I'm paying attention and acting, as a result, not so much from logic but more on guts. If it feels right, it's right. Do it. If there's a little voice that says "Run," I run. I think that certainly has served me well.

I don't, in any way, think anyone should try and discount that. I think women are a lot better at doing it than men are. I think they're much more likely to be tuned into their emotions and gut feelings and operate that way. I'm trying to develop it more and more all the time.

Nancy Currie

Astronaut

I always question things. I think it's the nature of my job to always question things. And I do sometimes have certain intuitions that, you know, something's just not right here. I used to question, whether it was a flight controller, or a maintenance guy trying to get me to fly the aircraft, or whatever. So I've learned not to have blind faith in things. Again, there's not much room for tolerance of error in a lot of the things we do. So it's not that I'm untrusting. It's just I feel it's part of our job to question everything.

Rabbi Stacy Friedman

Rabbi

Intuition? Definitely. It really fits into this other level of knowing and this other level of the universe that's taking place. There are a lot of things going on that we don't know about, and I think that we can be at certain levels or places where we connect to it.

To ask whether you believe in intuition is like asking whether you believe in your emotions. It's just a part of life. So I definitely do believe in it, and I think the more we trust intuition, the easier life can be.

Valerie Coleman Morris
Anchorwoman/TV personality

"Intuitive" has been the sort of word that has been maligned and used and hooked into 900 numbers in the psychic phenomenon. In pure form I do believe that we all have intuition and that it really is the inner voice in us speaking to us. We just ignore it so often and give authorship to someone else about thoughts that really could have begun in our own mind and in our own hearts.

So, yes, I trust in my intuition and instinct. Sometimes I'll just get a sense or a feeling. Last weekend I said to my nephew, who is going off for six weeks during the summer to work, "If there's something that you're about to do and it gives you pause and makes you think about it, listen to that and don't do it. Or if there's something that says you ought to do it and here's the reason why, then even if other people aren't signed on to what it is, listen to your intuition and be motivated by it." I do think there's an inner voice; it's just sometimes we alter what it's saying.

Sylvia Boorstein
Author/Educator/Lecturer

Intuition has not been a word that I think about a lot, because sometimes I have hunches, but the hunches are at least sometimes reflections of my tendency to have catastrophic mind states. So my "intuitions" are usually that something isn't going to work or isn't going to get better. It usually gives rise to a fear, and the fear contracts the mind, and then I'm in worse shape.

I'm more of a thinker than an intuitive type, although contemplative practice is an intuitive practice. I think of myself as an intuitive because I love contemplative practice, but that's not so much going on hunch, if that is the sort of intuition you mean. In the meditation practice that I do, you really don't make something happen; you stay alert for what is happening. A friend of mine had the best line. He said, "You don't do a particular thing. You don't invoke or breathe in a particular way or do certain things. You don't condition the mind state. You just wait to see what happens." He said it's really like a prayer. It's like one of the Catholic abandonment prayers where you say, "Here I am, God. Do whatever you want to me. It's up to you." To that degree I'm an intuitive.

Reverend Veronica Goines
Presbyterian pastor

I would probably have a lot of different names for it, but I think it's all a part of how God speaks to us. I think it's all about how God guides our lives, and a lot of people don't even recognize that that's what's happening. A lot of times we don't recognize when it's happening, but I believe it plays a big role.

When I was in my second marriage and about to leave my career to go into seminary to begin a whole other career, I just knew in myself. I can't explain to people to this day how there are times that I just know things. It's a spirit thing, and that's what intuition is—a spirit thing. It's not just a matter of instinct or whatever. I think it's very spiritually based, that it is one of the ways God accesses us and is able to guide and direct us if we learn to trust it. Early on in my life I didn't always trust it, but I'm learning more and more to trust it and not give it so much time that I have to go through a lot of unnecessary stuff before I finally believe it. It's like I hear it now and say, "Yeah, I'm going with it." I believe in it and rarely is it off.

I think that women especially are taught not to trust it. It's so diminished. We may say, "I'm not feeling comfortable about this," and we know in our gut it's not really the right thing to do. The truth is that something is registering. But we may be taught, "Oh, you just worry too much." So after a while it's been pushed down and stepped on and dismissed so many times that we learn not to trust it. But as little children we do trust it and go with it. We learn not to, and then we have to relearn.

Marti McMahon

Entrepreneur

Yes, I absolutely believe in intuition. And I put a lot of confidence into it. I may be off base once in a while, but I feel that you just follow your heart, and I place a lot of stock in it. If it just doesn't feel right, don't do it.

Jo Hanson

Artist/Environmentalist

I have a lot of confidence in it. It's the one thing you have to have in art, because art is guided a lot by intuition. It's intuition that tells you when something works and when it doesn't. It suggests to you ways to deal with it and tells you when to stop.

I think of intuition as guidance, and I feel my guidance is good whether it's for parking or doing artwork. I'm very grateful for my guidance. Part of my formal education and spiritual systems have to do with the relationship of the conscious mind and what we call the superconscious or high self, or whatever, and the subconscious mind. In the system that I studied, it's considered that there has to be a good relationship among these minds in order for the communication to be good. In particular, the subconscious mind is a sort of transfer station. If you want communications to go through these various forms of consciousness or whatever name you use for it, the subconscious mind has to be agreeing. So your job is to clear the things that trouble your subconscious mind or make it feel not worthy or stubborn and resentful. When you succeed in doing that, then your inner communication works well, and that to me is a significant part of one's guidance. That's the way I look at intuition.

Mary Bitterman
President/CEO, public television

I think there's a lot to be said for intuition. Not everything is perfectly clear, especially in the complicated societies with which we find ourselves dealing today.

I don't claim to have any special strength of intuitive talent. My husband thinks I'm quite intuitive. But I think part of intuition is derived from listening, from taking a lot in. The opposite occurs if you're always emoting, and are always being the one talking, and always giving your point of view without benefiting from the thoughts of others, from the wisdom of others, from witnessing how people deal with different circumstances and challenges. If you take a lot in, I think over time that helps to give you a repertoire from which you can derive some intuition, which can be very helpful.

Jeanne Rizzo
Entrepreneur

Absolutely I believe in intuition. Of course. And when I don't use it, when I defy it, when I compartmentalize it, when I push it away, I can feel it and I know it.

I think that we don't acknowledge what we call intuition in women, and I think men unfortunately haven't been given an opportunity to develop their intuition. Christopher and I have an agreement that if one of us feels that something is unsafe, whether it's getting on a plane or anything, that we will talk with each other about that. There have been times when he's said, "I really don't want you to take the bus today to the airport. I just don't feel good about that." Then we can explore that feeling. I wanted to help him develop intuition and separate it from fear. Because I think sometimes there are fear things, and that's why there's a judgment about intuition, because it gets confused with fear. You have to really understand what intuition is and what feelings you have that are conflicts or unresolved issues that you are putting in that language. But when I really have a sense about a person or a situation, I listen to it. I think the most important thing is to give that space, and if that means that I interrupt what I'm doing or interrupt the decision, I will try to do it. So I totally give credence to intuition.

Chapter 10

Chance and Luck

Karma is a better word to me than luck. I do believe that
karma carries with it a whole sense of spirituality, a sense of
practicality, a sense of reality, a sense of the intent of the content of who you are.

Valerie Coleman Morris

What role do chance and luck play in the lives of successful women? Do they make their own luck, or are they blessed by good
fortune that came to them for no apparent reason at all?

The women I spoke with have a variety of perspectives on these
questions. Some believe firmly in the power of chance, while others
just as firmly deny it. Some see in apparent chaos a hidden design. But
all agreed that, whatever chance befalls us, we always have it in our
power to choose how to respond to our circumstances.

Isabel Allende
Author

What roles have chance and luck played in my life? All kinds of roles. I work very hard. I'm very disciplined, but I'm very lucky. Bad luck and good luck. I can't determine what will happen. I'm given the cards, and the cards are marked. Now I try to play my game the best I can. But the cards are given.

Why do things happen? I wrote *The House of the Spirits* and that was work, discipline. I achieved something. But then it was good luck that it was rejected by every single publishing house in Latin America. I was forced to send it to an agent in Spain, who happened to be the best agent for Latin American literature in the world. And it's bad luck that she receives one thousand manuscripts per week. And it's good luck that I was a woman, and that I was Latin American and my name was Allende. She read it because of the name. It was good luck that she decided to take me and launch the book. And it was also good luck that she took the book to the Frankfurt Fair in Germany that year and all the European publishers wanted to buy it.

So there are things that I don't determine, they just come. It was good luck that I met Willie in that lecture ten years ago. And bad luck that my daughter died.

So there is luck. I do believe in chance very strongly. But I also believe we have to grab the chances when they come, the good ones.

Lynn Woolsey

Congresswoman

I've made use of luck. I call it timing. I've had extremely good timing, and it can be on little or big things. For one, deciding to run for Congress—the timing was perfect. I would have never run against Barbara Boxer. Nobody would have.

I lived at the time in the very northern edge of her congressional district. I had to wait and see what happened with the redistricting. They drew that district without me in mind, believe me. Yet I would swear that if you throw a dart, my house is in the center of that district. It became mine, and I ran against eight other people for the primary, but I was in the best position by far. I had sixty percent of the vote and had worked in the county that votes the most and it was my seat. It was mine to be. It was mine to earn and do a good job of.

It's not that I think things like that are handed to you. I think there are reasons for people to vote for me. But if it had stayed with part of the district in San Francisco like it originally was, and me living on the outer edge, I couldn't have run. Nobody in San Francisco was going to vote for somebody from Petaluma. They would now because they know my record, but they wouldn't have then. That's luck and timing. And taking a risk. It's "Don't dilly-dally around and say I'll wait until next time." There was not going to be another time.

Carmel Greenwood
Entrepreneur

I believe you create your own reality. And make your own luck. I went to a public school in Australia. I didn't go to university. I worked in the Hong Kong Bank as a secretary. Then all of a sudden I'm a successful stockbroker, and people were saying, "You're just lucky." No, I'm not lucky, I created my luck. The job I got at the brokerage — three of my girlfriends had been there, and they lasted two days because they worked for a boss who yelled and screamed. I needed the money so desperately I stayed. I let the yells and screams come over my head and said, "No, I won't leave. I need the money. I'll put up with it because this is my power." So I've put up with a lot of things in my life, and I've created my own luck.

It was very difficult. First of all, I was a woman. And I could hardly add two and two together. But I was leaving my first husband. I desperately needed money, so I just studied. My husband was saying, "Oh, you're no fun anymore, you don't go out." And I didn't; I studied. And I failed the exam three times.

After the first time, friends said, "It serves you right. Who do you think you are?" You know? It was like, "You're thirty-seven, your life is finished. Who do you think you are?" It reminded me of my mother, who always said, "Who do you think you are?" [Laughter]

Then my second husband, John, when I said, "I failed!" said, "Well, take it again. Now you know so much more!" I said, "Well, yes, I do, I'll take it again." And I failed again.

By that time I had learned how to meditate, and I dropped a lot of beliefs about myself. That was when I got into spirituality and meditation, so I reprogrammed my brain as to who I was. That's how I did it. So what I presented was success, and that was only because the way I was thinking now was very different. I created a tape, "Creating the Powerful and Positive Person," and I listened to that tape in the morning and the evening. It told me how wonderful I was! [Laughter] And slowly my mother's voice saying, "Who do you think you are?" got off my back, and I presented an image of being successful.

When I finally got my stockbroker's license, my boss said, "That's great. How are you going to get clients?" And I thought, "I'll have a radio program." And I phoned up my friend who was on the radio, Maggie Britain, and we had lunch. I said, "How would you like to have a radio program about finance?" She said, "I can't add two and two together." I said, "That makes two of us, but I'll give you the questions to ask and I'll answer them! Then we'll have people phoning in, and if we don't know the answer, I'll get back to them!" [Laughter] So that's how I formed my client list.

Then, because I was so up-front and honest about finance, I had men coming in, whose brother or best friend maybe worked at Merrill-Lynch, and I said, "Doesn't your brother or your friend work at Merrill-Lynch?" They said, "Yes, but I don't know what he's talking about! I can ask you a question, and you'll tell me honestly what it's about." So that's how I gained clients—because I told the truth.

I didn't go to Eton, I didn't go to Cambridge, but I did have integrity, and I think that's how I made it. When I first went to Hong Kong, I met a guy called Benny Wu, and I taught him how to scuba dive. I never inquired into what people had; it never meant anything to me. So when I got my stockbroker license fifteen years later, he walked in the door in his jeans, and I said, "Have a coffee," and he wrote a check for a million dollars. I tore it up and threw it in the garbage bin and said, "Don't be so funny!" He said, "No, you can cash it!" And he smiled and said, "You never knew my family, did you?" It turned out he was Gordon Wu's brother in Hong Kong.

So I think because I've just been who I am, and taken risks, that's how I made it. I never listened to everybody tell me that I couldn't do it. If somebody said I couldn't do it, it was like red flag to a bull. And when my first husband said he'd see me in the gutter, it was like a red rage came up: "We'll see who sees who in the gutter!" [Laughter] All my life it's been like that. If someone says I can't do it, then it's like "Well, why not?"

So, perseverance, integrity, and a dream: a dream that anyone can do it.

Gretchen Dewitt
Public relations professional

I feel that I have made things happen. My strongest sense of that was my first trip to Egypt. I felt that I could make anything happen, that I could almost make people say certain things. I remember I had met an Egyptologist, and we had a little game of saying, "We're going to meet this person, and we are going to think certain thoughts, and then we'll make this person say this thing." And I thought I was making things happen in Egypt. Part of that was Egypt. I felt that there was a residue of magic still, that I almost felt it in the air, that there was a dust left over from thousands of years ago when this civilization was producing everything—religion, art, magic, architecture, mathematics, agriculture—everything. There was still some magic in the air for me. There was a real sense of spirituality from Egypt, and I felt that I could make things happen, see what I wanted to see, have an event take place.

I don't know about chance and luck. Those words are elusive for me. I think that life is sometimes accidental and sometimes not, that we send out vibes, we send out signals to people. And I believe that we have choice, and I also believe the choice is limited. We are restricted in our choices by our emotional and our physical backgrounds. I was restricted in who I could choose, for example, for a first husband, because I had had a certain kind of father, and I was seeking, unbeknownst to me, resolution, and looking for what was familiar. So choice is limited, but we do have choice.

I think people have more power than perhaps they are aware of as far as making things happen in their lives. I think that just to put a certain expression on one's face can make things happen one way or another. So chance and luck? I think we have to depend more on ourselves than on chance and luck.

Alice Waters
Restaurateur/Author/Educator

I've been very lucky. But I think it has a lot to do with timing. In that sense, you do make your luck. You just feel that it's the right time for something. Intuition is there, but it's really timing, because I know so many people who have had wonderful ideas, and they just came too soon. And they didn't happen.

There's a lot of being willing to reach out to people and test the waters. I ask a lot of questions to a lot of people—what do you feel about this, what do you feel about that. Some people think I ask too many questions, because I can't make up my own mind. But I ask those questions until I get an answer that makes sense to me. And I just don't stop. I'll ask and ask and ask and ask. I may even ask twenty-five people, because I want it to fit right.

Rosie Casals
Professional athlete

I do believe you make your luck. But also there are times that things are beyond your control. Like winning Grand Slam events, winning important matches. Sometimes it's luck. Somebody's not playing well, and you're playing great. Conditions are right. You've got to be at the right place at the right time. I do believe that. I do believe in some destiny and some luck, because there have been situations where things have been so close. The ball could have been out. It could have bounced on your side. And that was the difference in that match. It wasn't anything more than that. It wasn't that your opponent was better, or you were worse. So I do believe in luck, and that you make your own luck, and that sometimes it just happens without you ever having a part of it.

Elizabeth Colton

Entrepreneur

The other day I was looking for a way to meet more international people, so I joined this group called the World Affairs Council, which hosts programs, and I happened to be reading about the president of the Council, who is a very accomplished woman, and I realized that I went to school with her. So is that chance and luck? Partially, but is it also the fact that I'm making my own chance and luck at researching these opportunities and going out and seeking out this group? Meeting you today. Is that chance and luck, or is that because I went out and sought out Mary Bitterman? So it's kind of like intuition. Maybe partly there is some kind of fate or chance, but certainly it's driven by how we set ourselves up for those opportunities and how we invest in what we're doing and the energy we bring to it.

I think that sometimes your friendships are based on opportunity. I had a friend once when I lived in New York who maybe under normal circumstances I wouldn't have necessarily become friends with, but at the time we were both working on the same project and we each found each other because we had a need for a friend at the time, and we became good friends and we still are. That was a kind of chance. So I think sometimes things are developed from chance and opportunity. But it's really driven by how you are investing in yourself and your life.

Sue Backman

Entrepreneur/Billiards professional

I don't believe in such a thing as chance. The concept just doesn't exist. I think everything happens because you create it, and luck is simply what happens when you create something in a positive way for yourself.

Some people would say I'm lucky. I can give them equal amount of times where I haven't been. So I think it's really paying attention to intuition, taking advantage of opportunities, and being able to rise above difficulty and things that would block success. I think as I've gotten older I've gotten better at doing that.

Nancy Currie

Astronaut

As I said earlier, there was nobody more surprised than me when I got picked for this job, so I think it was truly a matter of the right place at the right time. I don't know if somebody was watching out for me or if it was just pure luck. But I think, generally speaking, I've been exceptionally lucky in my life.

I think the people who know me would tell you that I make my luck. Because of the way I look at life, I'd just say that I'm lucky. I look at the people around me, and I see their qualifications, and I'm just overwhelmed. Never did I think that I would be in their company. And I think sometimes people look at me and say, "Well, look at all these qualifications that you have." I don't have the ability to see that.

Valerie Coleman Morris
Anchorwoman/TV personality

I think it is hard for any person of color in this country and in many countries around the world to ever say that what happened to us was just lucky. Life has had to be more deliberate than that.

Karma. Karma is a better word to me than luck. I do believe that karma carries with it a whole sense of spirituality, a sense of practicality, a sense of reality, a sense of the intent of the content of who you are.

I do think you can impact your own karma. I think it's reciprocity. If you do good deeds and think as clearly as you can, if your motivation is logical and thought out and you're being proactive rather than reactive, I think that your karma will be better. How good it is depends on how hard you work at it.

I think there are a lot of people who think, "If I'm an okay person, then everything should be okay." That would be wonderful, but life just isn't that way. My grandmother would say, "You have to make a way out of no way." There are no shortcuts. She filled me with that. My grandmother filled me with those things because her children and her grandchildren and great-grandchildren were the hope of the things she wasn't ever able to accomplish. So she gave us the sum total of her philosophies all the time, and they were good. "Make a way out of no way." She would say, "The elevator to success is broken. You've got to take the stairs." She would say, "If you don't stand for something, you'll fall for anything." If you think about those sayings, they're all very logical, and they give you a very focused and realistic course.

Sylvia Boorstein
Author/Educator/Lecturer

I've had a lot of good luck. I think my life has been very blessed. I've had good health. Some of my children have actually had quite difficult health problems. But, thank God, we're all alive and nobody is tremendously physically compromised or any other kind of compromised.

Even meeting my husband was great luck. It's hard to know when you're young what's of value. It's hard to know when you're young what's going to be a match or what's going to last forever. So it's really a lot of luck.

It depends on who I'm talking to. If I'm talking to Buddhists, I say that I've got a lot of good merit karma. If I'm talking to Jews, I say God and all my ancestors are looking after me. It's just a vocabulary.

Reverend Veronica Goines

Presbyterian pastor

I don't believe in chance or luck at all. I believe everything is ordained—whatever happens in my life, the good and the bad. Not that I believe God causes the bad, but I believe that God is still able to operate and work in it and bring something good of it. So in that respect I really don't base my life on luck at all. There is a real sense of God's providence at work.

I've defined providence for the congregation as God's hand in the glove of circumstances. I believe that God does operate that way in our lives. Generally we don't see it so clearly until after the fact. That has been my experience—not necessarily being aware at the time, but being able to look back and say, "I do see that."

I think we learn a lot more sometimes from the real challenges in our lives. I also believe that God opens doors for us that no one else can close and that God can close doors in our lives that no matter what we do we can't open. The thing is to live our lives in such a way that we are so into doing what pleases God, which really is what brings us joy. So it's to live our lives that way and then just to watch God open doors and watch God do things in our lives and use us as instruments in this world beyond anything we can imagine.

Marti McMahon

Entrepreneur

I think your eyes have to be open and you have to look for opportunities. Yes, there are chances out there, but if your eyes are closed you won't see them. As far as luck is concerned, I think luck can work if you're willing to work hard at making that luck work. I put more stock into hard work and not taking no for an answer and just finding solutions as to how to make something work. I believe more in that.

I also strongly believe in passion. I'm a very passionate person, and I feel that anyone can be successful if they find something that they are passionate about. Sometimes you're just going down the wrong path and that's why chance, or luck, or whatever, isn't there for you — because you're not in the right place. To me, I've been lucky that I did find my passion, and that's one of the reasons why I feel that I'm successful.

I think, too, that when you have that passion, you're willing to work all the hours it takes to make it work because your passion gives you stamina. It gives you that energy. I used to work one hundred hours a week, many, many, many weeks. But I didn't feel it. Oh, I was tired. I was so tired sometimes I would sit down and say, "I can't go on," and cry. But I'll tell you, I was passionate about what I was doing, and I just picked myself up and woke up the next morning and did it again.

Jo Hanson

Artist/Environmentalist

I don't feel that chance exists. I think that in everything that one does the conditions for the other things are being created. This obviously becomes a very complex web of positive elements. But I think that you're setting up everything that flows in your life, and, of course, you're setting it up relative to very complex systems that are outside also. But in the web in which everything is connected there is a knowledge that's not conscious knowledge of what leads to what and how things combine. I feel that you set up what you need, and if you need to do certain learning that you've been backward about, you may injure your back and it may take you through things that provide very valuable learning. What I mean to be saying is that things you may regard as misfortune are not. They're not chance. Putting all the elements together is the way to get to your own learning system and open up experiences and open up learning and perception.

Mary Bitterman

President/CEO, public television

I'm Irish; my maiden name is Foley. They talk about the luck of the Irish, although the Irish sometimes, at least in poems and many songs, come across as a rather dour, sad people. The old saying is, "The fate of every Irishman is to know that one day life will break his heart." And there can be a lot of stout drinking over this, and poetry writing, and lots of other things. But there's also the gold at the end of the rainbow. So it's a kind of mixed set of allusions.

I think there's a good deal to be said about chance, and good luck, good fortune. I really do. And I think it goes back to the recognition that you don't do anything on your own. Part of what's brought to bear when you are successful is very often being in the right place at the right time, with the right people, and it's just a set of fortuitous events. I don't believe in any kind of predestination, that some people have the luck of the draw and some people don't. I earnestly believe in the potential of all people to affect their futures. I just don't like hearing people say, "There is nothing I can do about it." Because people have the most remarkable ability to change and to affect their own lives and those of others. And it's not people on some powerful dais. I see people every day, and the people who give me the greatest sense of hope for the future of mankind are really in large part very straightforward, day in, day out people, who go about their lives, lives that they would probably describe as unremarkable, in fairly remarkable ways. I look at women who are raising children, who are working, who are very often single parents, who bring a sense of perseverance, of stick-to-itiveness, of a sense of values, who contribute to making this society work. These are really the people who deserve special recognition, which is not always accorded them.

I have been so lucky to have wonderful parents, wonderful grandparents, a terrific husband, a very idiosyncratic, creative, terrific daughter, wonderful friends. That's where the luck is. Because it's those people who give you the sort of sustenance that one needs to live an energetic, demanding life in such a way as to retain perspective and retain a joyfulness in very difficult and sad times as well as in good times.

Sister Mary Neill

Nun/Author/Educator

I think luck and chance play every role. You know: How did Sylvia wind up in my class, and why did we become friends?

I went to Europe by mistake. I was set to go to the Jesuit School of Berkeley, and they lost my folder, so all of a sudden I'm on the plane to France. I'm thirty-eight years old. I do not speak French. I have not been accepted to the university. I've worn a medieval dress for twenty years. I haven't had money in my hand. I've never been on a plane or a train. And here I am getting on the plane and going to France, and my French is so bad that the French can't believe that anyone could speak French so badly. Of course, I taught Latin for sixteen years, and some guy had said, "Oh, Latin and French are the same." Ahh!

Steven Vey said that God comes through the gaps. For me, those are the accidents. I mean, if you said chaos theory, we're here on the Earth because of the gaps that happened, the way chaos comes. So I think it's everything.

I also think that it's very important to be very grateful. What I want to say at the end of my life is thank you, thank you. The story that I tell my students is of Gandhi, that when Gandhi looked up and saw the gun that was to kill him, he called the gun "God." He knew the gun was God. "Yes, thank you, there it is. It's coming."

Chance—you know, I tend to use more theological language, but I call it surprise and being grateful for surprise. I've been a really controlling woman. I'm very controlled. So I tried more to live with surprise. It gets unnerving, though.

Jeanne Rizzo

Entrepreneur

Chance and luck . . . It's a more complicated thing for me than—how do I explain this? There are people who believe, for example, that you bring on your own illness. Then there are all the people who have to feel awful and guilty because they're ill and they've brought that on. That's one extreme of that concept: making your luck or chance. I feel that the clearer and cleaner and more honest and sincere our energy is—and it takes work to clear out the stuff that is not clean—the more we will attract that other energy and we will attract things to us that will fulfill the destiny that we have. So is it really chance? Is it really luck? Those are two terms that I don't think apply in the spiritual life in the way that I understand it.

There are experiences sometimes that I have about which one might say, "That's bad luck. Why did that happen? Why did you get hit on the bridge by a drunk driver?" Well, that's no accident to me. I never called that an accident. I wouldn't call it luck or chance. I would call it a necessity in my time on this planet to meet something, and I did. It was an opportunity for me. I needed a wake-up call, and I got it. I had a choice of how to deal with it at that point. I think all the things we define as bad luck or bad chance—is there a reason defined by intellectual reason? No. Is there an opportunity to take that and do something with it? Absolutely.

You have all these women who are being subjected to environmental causes of their breast cancer. What did they do to deserve that? Is that bad luck? It's an opportunity for us to change how the world is viewed and in the big picture, in the whole length of the world, there are going to be an awful lot of women who have to die for that message to happen. My responsibility is not to miss that message. I hope that I'm not one of the women who is the one in eight who gets breast cancer and has to live with those bad decisions that were made about the air we breathe and the planet we walk on. But when that's happening, it's my opportunity to see that.

So I wouldn't put it in terms of chance or luck for me. I would put it more in terms of opportunities and challenges, and they are sometimes really hard. Looking back on my accident, which I call the wreck—I don't call it an accident—I am so much more of the person that I would have hoped to be today than I think I would have been if that hadn't happened. I can still feel the pain of it, but I welcome the opportunities that it gave me. So I don't have language that answers it exactly. That's how I live it.

Chapter 11

Maturity — At Any Age

Even though I'm forty-six years old, I don't have any problem
with getting down on the floor and crawling around with a
four-year-old, making noises, making faces . . . I'm not afraid
to be silly, to make jokes no matter what the situation is. The
worst thing, I think, would be to lose one's sense of humor
and take oneself too seriously.

Sue Backman

We all get older, if we are lucky. With advancing age come
many changes. Certainly our perceptions of ourselves and of what is
important in our lives change as we mature. But do we necessarily grow
wiser? Do we leave behind outmoded stages and perceptions, like but-
terflies emerging from their cocoons, or does our journey take us full
circle to a wisdom we possessed as children? And how do we accom-
modate ourselves to the physical and emotional changes that age

brings? How do we adjust to an ever-shortening future? Listen as the women in this chapter reflect on these questions, and draw from the gift of their experience as you strive to understand your own.

Isabel Allende
Author

Have I changed much over time? Physically, I have changed on the outside. Physically I look very different now but inside I'm very strong, I'm very healthy. I'm still physically able to do the same things I did when I was twenty, which is very good luck. But I know it won't last, because my husband is sixty and I know that he doesn't feel young anymore. He gets tired very easily. He wants to retire. He suffers terribly from jet lag. I don't suffer any of those things yet, but I know they will come.

Getting older has meant strength, incredible strength for me. Because I have a wonderful bullshit detector! I know exactly what you have to discard from your life. It would be very easy for a person in my position to believe my own press clippings and start believing in success, for example, and start playing the celebrity thing because everything is given for me to do that. But because I have failed too many times and I have lost everything so many times, I know that it will last for a time and then it will be gone. In very little time people won't even remember my name or who I am. Because this is the nature of life. Everything passes. The fact that today I sell millions of books doesn't mean anything. In twenty years maybe they will have been totally forgotten, and I have to be able to live with that. So this is what age has done for me. When I was twenty-five or thirty and I was a successful journalist in Chile, I thought I was a celebrity. I lived the role, and I thought it was great, and I felt so fantastic. Now I don't get anything from that.

I don't believe that love will last forever, therefore I enjoy it when I have it. I enjoy health because I have it, but I know it won't last. I enjoy my son as much as I can because something can happen. The same with my grandchildren.

So getting older has meant strength, detachment, being open to all the experiences, the good and the bad, not being afraid. I've lost the fear of death, therefore I'm afraid of very few things. I'm not afraid of old age. I'm afraid of deteriorating too much in the last stage of life. I suppose that happens because one needs to go through that to learn something. I've always said that I will kill myself before I let that happen, but that's an act of arrogance, of being a controlling bitch, of trying to control even death. Maybe there is something to learn in that deterioration. Maybe there is a reason why my daughter needed to be in a coma for a year and be paralyzed and in a vegetative state for a year. Maybe her spirit needed to learn something. Who am I to decide, to determine that?

Lynn Woolsey

Congresswoman

My grandmother died when she was sixty-three, and my mother died when she was sixty-two, and my sister died when she was fifty-seven. I'm sixty-one. I'm not dying. I have no intentions of dying. I have no women in my family to show me how older women are in my family and that it's okay to get old. I feel an emptiness about that. I'll do it on my own. I'll forge it in our family. It's frightening.

I figure I'll live at least another twenty years. I've got so much to do after I'm sixty-five. I'm just starting, and that's part of it. I live a fairly healthy life. I don't smoke or drink a bunch or anything like that. But I know that wisdom comes with age, and I respect older women. I love older women. It's the third piece of your life. First is youth, then young women raising families, and then women with wisdom. I want to earn that and love it and try it.

I'm enjoying it more and more. If I looked at me through my mother's eyes, who would have rather been dead than get old, then I'd be a mess. What an awful way to be. I don't color my hair because I just decided I'm not going to do that. It's okay hair, and I would if I wanted to. It's not that I don't think I can. There are just things that she would have done that I don't do because I don't need to. I don't want people to think that because I don't color my hair I'm wise. The two don't equate at all.

Gretchen Dewitt
Public relations professional

Well, I know some foolish old people. So, does wisdom come with maturity? It would really be perverse not to know more as one got older. It should be a reward for not looking quite as wonderful.

My perceptions toward life? I am so surprised that I am as old as I am. I remember sobbing when I turned thirty, thinking how could I possibly be this old. I wish someone had told me that I wasn't old at all. Now, when I think how could I possibly be this old, I say to myself, "Think that you're young, because at eighty-five you will have been young at this age."

What has changed in my life? I don't know what has changed in my life. I try not to waste time. I think I wasted more time when I was young because I thought there was more time. So I waste less time, because I know that life will not be lying on the beach trying to get a tan in the summer.

I am more patient, because impatience never got me anything. I can remember as a teenager feeling cross, and as a very young adult, feeling annoyed. And really, I have given that up. I much prefer feeling amused or happy. And nothing's really worth it. There are just so few things that are really worth bad feelings that I have eliminated that mostly from my life.

Also, I can remember thinking as a very young person, "Oh, I don't like so and so," or "I don't want to talk to so and so." And I remember going on a safari to East Africa, where I was thrown together with a group of people, and some of them were monsters. But I was stuck with them. I was twenty-six. And at that point in my life, I thought, "I'm stuck with them, so I'm going to find something good or interesting about this person. I'm going to give this person an opportunity to shine, to be a wonderful person." It was a challenge, and it was a game. There's no way to lose that game, because there's always something that someone will want to talk about that's interesting or pleasant.

The challenge is to find that in everybody. As a young, young person, I didn't do that. I was lazy about it. I simply wouldn't have been bothered. I bother now, because it's so good for the other person, and it's good for me.

So those are some changes. I'm wiser, now that I'm older. But I'm not sure that happens to everybody.

Alice Waters
Restaurateur/Author/Educator

I think that we have to learn how to live a lot more consciously. What I regret is that I lived pretty unconsciously for a very long time. I feel like only now have I awakened. And all the time is gone.

I think kids have to be encouraged at a very early age. It's important to teach kids that they need to follow their inner voices. They need to do things that are good for themselves, to really get connected with that part of themselves early on. They can get very swept away. I know teenage kids are so sensitive that way, and so influenced. They have to be reminded that they have something special and that they can succeed in whatever endeavor they choose, but they have to be very true to themselves. I'm still struggling with that with my teenage daughter, helping her try and find her way. It takes a lot of time, and you have to give them a lot of time. They need it.

Rosie Casals
Professional athlete

I think that when you're young, you just bounce back. You make decisions, and you always think there's time, there's time. As you get older, you know there's not the time. Time goes by quicker and quicker. As I get to fifty, I realize that time is now. So I try and do the things that are important to me, and see the people that I need to see now. Because tomorrow could be too late. You just never know where you're going to be tomorrow.

Elizabeth Colton
Entrepreneur

I think wisdom definitely comes with maturity; it's just a question of when we reach maturity, if ever. [Laughter]

I think we definitely gain perspective as we get older. I am certainly no exception to the rule of being a very progressively liberal person when I was younger and as I'm older I still hold on very firmly to the social beliefs, but I probably have tempered the economic ones. Let's just say I've broadened my view of the world so I understand a lot of different realities and that everything isn't black and white and that there are a lot of different forces at work in any one situation and we need to understand them all.

I think we certainly gain wisdom from our life experiences. I think one of the hardest parts is to gain wisdom when you're dealing in an emotional way with the opposite sex or whoever is a love interest in your life. I hope that we learn from those experiences, but I sometimes think those are the hardest ones to learn from.

Understanding the value of friendship is something I think we gain with maturity. Knowing the place that friends can play in our life. Understanding our responsibilities to the next generation.

If you learn from your experiences, then you are getting wiser as time goes on. I think that's the key: just to learn from your experiences and to always be open-minded to learning, whether it be learning from people, from different cultures, or from people who have different experiences than yours. You have to value and respect all different kinds of people to be open to learning from them. I think that's part of it too.

Annelies Atchley
Educator/Artist

Yes. Wisdom comes with experience. It comes with the openness to be yourself and to serve others. If you're into yourself too much—this sounds totally ridiculous, but I'm sincere that I'm as far away from the Big Bang as an ant. So I don't think I'm worth more in this world than an ant. That's why I never got along with Christianity very well, because they always think they're better than anybody else. I think I'm not better than a deer on a hill. I don't think I'm better than a stone on the street, because I'm as far away from the Big Bang. I do think I have intelligence, which is not my doing. I can see better and hear better than a stone. All those are things that were given to me without me having to do anything for it.

I'm basically a server, and in serving I found a lot of freedom. If I give a child the best day or best drawing they can have, I see the happiness come back to me from that child and I'm happy. Or if I go in a post office and there's a grumpy person who has been there for days and has had a bad day, I always go in and think, "How can I make her smile?" I say, "You must have had a bad day, but you know what? In about an hour you'll be off, and you can have a nice glass of wine." Ultimately they always smile, and I feel good, but they feel good too.

That's what service to others is. It also makes you understand others, and once you understand others and have compassion for others and animals and everything, you can feel their spirits. Wisdom comes through spiritual guidance or sensitivity.

I have said things lately that I heard myself saying and said, "Where did that come from?" For instance, a little girl took a bead from me at a birthday party. She told the father at home, who thought it would be good if the child would bring it back. He was out of town, so she had to wait two weeks. Finally he brought her, and he stayed in the car while she talked to me. She said, "This is something that is yours." I said, "How did you get it?" She said, "I took it." I said, "How did you know how to bring it back?" She said, "I told my daddy." Then I said, "Was it your heart that told you?" "Oh, yes. I was tossing and turning and couldn't sleep all night." So I said, "You're a very special girl that you listen to your heart. Girls who listen to their heart are so special, and they are people I want to know."

We had this whole conversation about the heart, and her eyes opened and she stayed and made a necklace and a doll, and we became very good friends. The father absolutely was enchanted. That kind of wisdom came from thirty years of teaching children and appreciating things and showing them things. That's wisdom that makes me totally appreciate being older.

When other things fall apart, you have to learn to look at the good in yourself and say, "Look. This is what I lost, but this is what I gained." When you're younger, you have to look at that: "This is what I don't have yet, but this is what I have." If you do that in your life and say, "I'm doing the best job where I am, where nature puts me," then wisdom comes automatically. If you're a frog and you do the best as a frog, you're a wise frog. If as a person you do the best you can, you're a wise person.

Laurel Burch

Artist

My honest opinion about maturity is that it's not a given. When I see people, the number of years they've lived has nothing to do with their wisdom. It's just awesome to me that somebody can be five or six years old and be wiser than mature adults I know. So I'm not sure where it does come from, but I know that it doesn't come just with age.

I honestly think that my own wisdom has come because of my

wanting it. I seek it. I want to learn, I want to understand. Sometimes I take the harder route because of the value that I place in the wisdom. There are so many times in life when you can choose a path that is so much easier, but the richness, by comparison, is not the same.

I don't mean that I choose a harder path for the sake of choosing a harder path. I mean I place such a high value on wisdom that if I think there's more to learn by going a certain way or exploring something, it's riskier, it's unknown, but I'll usually do that. I go in that direction hoping that something will contribute to wisdom.

Personally, I do feel wiser the older I get. But I don't think it comes in general with age.

Sue Backman

Entrepreneur/Billiards professional

I probably have a little bit different take on getting older or younger than most people. I think that as you get older you don't necessarily have to age. In some ways what I've been trying to do is get younger as I get older, which maybe sounds a little crazy. Even though I'm forty-six years old, I don't have any problem with getting down on the floor and crawling around with a four-year-old, making noises, making faces . . . I'm not afraid to be silly, to make jokes no matter what the situation is. The worst thing, I think, would be to lose one's sense of humor and take oneself too seriously. So I've really tried not to do that.

I don't necessarily think that wisdom comes with maturity. It can, but some of the wisest people I know are three years old and some of the most idiotic people that I know are in their seventies. So it can go both ways. I think some people get less wise as they get older, and some manage to still learn. I don't think it's necessarily related to your age, per se. Some people are born wise, and if they're lucky they don't lose that wisdom.

Nancy Currie

Astronaut

I think there are certain things that happen in your life that cause you to be mature. I think that because of some things that happened early on in my life I matured a bit sooner than most. Most twenty-year-olds don't come to grips with their own mortality when they see something like an accident or whatever. I think that coming to grips with that causes you to mature. It causes you also to look at your life and say what's important.

One of the things that hit me is, my father had a triple bypass about ten years ago. He was one of these guys who always worked—you know, the company came first. He either lived in another city half the time or he was always on the road, and never at the activities that we were participating in. He really gave everything to his company. And when he had his heart attack and had this bypass, it wasn't the folks from his company who were sitting next to his bedside in the hospital, holding his hand. It was his family. I think he saw that for the first time.

I think maybe that changed my perspective on life, although my husband would probably be the first to tell you I'm a workaholic. But I really do try to put my family first, because they are what's important. If

I had to rank, it's God, family, job. Hopefully I'm not slighting any of those. It's always a very tough balance. But hopefully my family knows full well that I put them ahead of anything, and that I'd do anything for them. Some people, in the quest to have a great profession, maybe lose sight of that. They think either they can't have a family or they can't have a very good relationship with their family because they're too busy working. But if you think, if something catastrophic happened in your life, who would be there to help you, it's going to be your family. Family and friends.

Rabbi Stacy Friedman
Rabbi

I spent a lot of my life working with older people. Before I became a rabbi, I worked in a nursing home and spent a lot of time with older people. And I think wisdom definitely comes from maturity and confidence.

I lead a monthly women's spirituality group, and it's intergenerational, so there are women from their twenties through their nineties. It's the most wonderful thing, and I think the most wonderful thing about it is what the younger women learn from the older women. When somebody comes with some kind of problem or issue, the older women say, "You know what? I've been through that, and this is what I did, and this is what I'm doing now." It's so inspirational.

But I've also seen how old age can be devastatingly difficult for many people for financial or health reasons or loneliness. So wisdom definitely comes with maturity, but I don't think we can idealize old age, because it can be very difficult for some people.

Valerie Coleman Morris
Anchorwoman/TV personality

The wisdom of adjusting and amending is probably the greatest lesson I've learned as I've gotten older. That which we said we were going to do, we did. That which we wanted to accomplish and didn't, we shouldn't view as failures. I've heard a lot of people say, "I've made a mistake." I always like to say that was just a missed take, as opposed to a mistake, which is bad and negative. Without errors in what we're doing, we can't figure out what we really want to do. It's like when we talk to young people and say that if anybody in this television broadcasting business says they haven't been fired, they're either not telling you the truth or their career has been very guarded and circumspect. Because we all get fired in this business, and it isn't because we're bad. I've been fired, and they said: "It has nothing to do with you, Valerie. Your work is absolutely great. We are just going in a different direction." Wisdom said you accept that and don't go searching around asking "What did I do wrong? Why me?"

Wisdom also gave me the opportunity and the permission to have a pity party. I think pity parties are very important. I think it's important that we give ourselves permission to say, "I'm a mess. I'm a wreck. I have no idea what I'm going to do next, and therefore I'm going to have a pity party." Pity parties for me include no one but myself. They are definitely controlled in length of time. It is usually for one evening. When I go to bed I have in my mind, if not on paper, a list of what I'm going to do when I get up so that the pity party always has a prescribed beginning, middle, and end. It makes me feel a whole lot better. And in pity parties that's when you're going to say, "I'm really a nice person, I'm great at what I was doing, that made no sense that they did what they did and what happened." Whatever the negatives that you're feeling, whether it's in business or you're in the midst of divorce, in the midst of something negative happening with your child. Whatever may be going on, I'll throw a pity party if I need it because I'd much rather keep myself company in my anxiety and admit it to myself and put myself back together with a plan than go around saying, "I'm okay."

I'm tired of people who say, "Just shake it off. Have a stiff upper lip and move ahead." That's not female. We have almost tribal ways. I think that women are far more tribal in many ways than we'd like to believe in modern society. When I say tribal, I mean that we have rituals and we have processes that we go through. Some women may linger in them too long, but the reality of it is we do have a process. We have a beginning, middle, and end, and that completes the circle.

So in this process with me, I have found that I give permission for me to say, "That's what I thought then, and this is what I think now." Wisdom and experience and change of circumstances and changes of need offer me the opportunity to change what I'm doing and change my direction. It's not flighty, it's not female and vagrant. It's very vibrant, and there's nothing wrong with that.

Sylvia Boorstein
Author/Educator/Lecturer

I hope wisdom comes with maturity. We tend to say that as you get older you get wiser, but not everybody. You get kvetchier—grumpier.

One of the things that came up yesterday in talking with a friend about getting older is that we are no longer talking hypothetically about things past. My back is not as good as it used to be. My health is good, but I used to be able to sit for hours and meditate and my back won't support that anymore. I have to sit in a chair. Your parts don't work the same.

When I was twenty, my whole life was stretched out ahead of me. I'm sixty-three now, and I think, "Wow. I don't have a whole life stretching out ahead of me." In fact what it does is it inspires me, because who knows how long I'll live? Maybe I'll live quite a while yet, but at this point I'm still thinking very well and think I have some good things to say and teach. So I feel quite inspired to teach as much as I can for as long as I can while that part works. I have a certain zeal about thinking, especially as I see the body doesn't hold together exactly and I know it's got a finite shelf life. So I really have to teach as much as I can because I love feeling that I'm teaching something that is helpful to people. I feel I can't not give back. I am such a recipient of luck that I think the only response is to give it out.

Reverend Veronica Goines

Presbyterian pastor

I believe wisdom does come with maturity, but it doesn't necessarily come with physical age. Wisdom says that we're choosing to learn from life's challenges and mistakes, the goods and the bads. It really just means that we learn and take note as we go and then we can't help but grow in wisdom. But I do know that it's possible to live our lives bumping up against the same walls because we absolutely refuse to learn.

My perceptions toward life have changed and continue to change in many ways. As I get older, I find that there's not so much of a need for me to live my life so concerned about what other people think of me. I can be more true to myself. I live being more inwardly motivated as opposed to externally motivated, where I'm doing things so that I get applause or affirmations or something. It's very different, but it's liberating. As a woman in leadership, there are decisions that I have made and will make and am making now that aren't always perceived necessarily with enthusiasm. But if I'm really clear that that's what I'm supposed to do, then I'm okay with that. That's one of the biggest changes.

Just recently I experienced something of that sort here at the church. There was a time when I would have been spinning around in circles and up nights trying to figure it out or rethinking or second-guessing myself. I just find that there's less of that for me. It's like striving to live life through that clarity and not making decisions that are based on fuzziness. When I get clarity, I make the decision. Once I do, it's like really trusting that.

Irene Zisblatt Zeigelstein
Holocaust survivor

In the early forties, I was a teenager without a teenage life. I thought about it all the time: what it is like to be just an average teenager. I am a Holocaust survivor of the deadliest concentration camp in Auschwitz. I was thirteen years old when I was forced into this camp. While in there, I had to become an adult in a hurry, or I would have been taken to my death in the gas chamber, for my jailers did not favor teenagers. I did not dare think of things like lipstick, perfume, pop music, sexy clothes, or being cool. My thoughts were about surviving in these unspeakable conditions without food, clothes, shoes, without my parents, siblings, or friends. And hard labor for twelve hours a day.

As I approached the age of fourteen, I had hopes of being free, but that was a dream. Much to my surprise, a couple of months later, my dream became reality. After I escaped from the horrors of the Nazis and hid in the forest of an unknown place, I was found and liberated by the American army. A soldier who picked me up from the ground looked at my sixty-kilo body and not so human-looking face, and he asked me, "How old are you?" I replied, "Fourteen years old." And he said, "In my country, a fourteen-year-old girl is a young lady, strong, beautiful, and sometimes in a teen magazine." I was very happy that Hitler did not succeed in denying other girls their teen years. I thought about that magazine about teenagers, and I was thanking God for being alive and free and hoping to have an opportunity to read such a magazine.

I sometimes still read the teenage magazine at my age, in my sixties. It makes me feel that I was a part of that life also. So I like to share my past with teenagers who are so lucky to have a teenage life in their teen years.

Marti McMahon

Entrepreneur

Wisdom does come with maturity. Absolutely. But wouldn't it be nice to be twenty years younger and have the maturity that I have now?

I have grown a lot. I have seen that. I'm really happy with who I am. I feel so confident, so happy with my environment, with what I've created. I enjoy life so much. Twenty years ago, twenty-five years ago, I don't know whether each day would be as precious as it is now. I don't think it would be. When I look at the sun now, when I look at the moon, when I look at the beautiful water and the skyline, I have so much more of an appreciation than I did way back then. And I can focus in on it more instead of being distracted all the time by so much stuff going around me. When you are younger, there seem to be so many things going on that you just don't focus in on some of the finer things in life. It's money, really. It's not what money can buy. It's just the beauty of our world and people around you.

Jo Hanson
Artist/Environmentalist

I think the primary experience is that when I was younger I needed to be sharp and incisive and ahead of everybody. I have evolved into a state of being in which I don't have to be ahead of everybody. I need to be clear in my thinking, but I don't necessarily have to be sharp about it.

But what I really think about aging—assuming that you age with an image of aging into wisdom, what I observe is that your mind becomes more interested in relationships and associating things, integrating things and having insights that bring the whole structure of your understanding of existence into a coherent understanding and a wider one.

For me, perspective keeps getting wider, and I love it. It's a very rewarding kind of change.

About the image of aging into wisdom: There's a powerful influence in our society. We read about the elders of certain cultures and how they are the wise guidance and are cherished and cared for and so on. In that kind of society I would assume that people have the expectation of aging into wisdom, because that's the model.

It has occurred to me in my observations that our society projects a different image. What I see is that the discussion is of needing care as you get older, needing a nursing home, needing managed care, and aging into senility or incompetence or whatever. Or aging into a walled-in community for elders if you've got enough money. There's very little mention made of aging into wisdom. Mainly you age into problems.

I think it's a very important thing to try and project the image that you want people to follow. You can't tell people they're going to age into senility and then get something contrary to that image except in people who know themselves well enough to not accept it.

I have very strong feelings about that because it's mainly women more than men who are pushed into this pattern. The pattern has a lot to do, I think, with profit making with the pharmaceutical companies and the nursing home industry. I feel that it's really significant for us somehow to find the means of projecting a more self-respecting and respecting image.

Mary Bitterman
President/CEO, public television

As I've gotten older, I think I just believe more strongly in what I believed all the way along. I think that's probably right. As I grow older, I become probably more concerned about the things that always concerned me. Because my life experience has included travel throughout the world and meeting people from so many different cultures and backgrounds, I have been led to see that many of these issues that have always concerned me are just so manifest everyplace. I'm really talking about man's inhumanity to man. War. Destruction. Racial, cultural, religious, ethnic prejudice. Lifestyle prejudice. The need to discriminate against, beat up, attack, or kill somebody whether the person is gay or lesbian, whether the person is of a different ethnic origin, whether the person is of a different religious orientation.

These things always bothered me. From the time I was a small child I hated to see people being cruel to people. I guess the longer I live, the more I've seen of it. And so it only deepens my sense of concern and feeling the need, in my own way, through what possibilities and vehicles are available to me, to try to have some modest impact on these issues.

Jeanne Rizzo

Entrepreneur

I do think wisdom comes with age. I think there's a certain amount of experience that you have to have and a certain process you have to have gone through to achieve that.

I also think people were put on this planet with gifts of wisdom. I have been with children whose wisdom has absolutely influenced me. I think what happens is we come in with it and then the world beats it out and you have to get it back. I think we come in with the ability to have wisdom and take the world in, and then we get trained out of our wisdom because it's not expeditious and it's not practical. So there's not an encouragement to go to the place where you sense your wisdom. It's considered arrogance. So we train everybody out of it and then we all go to therapy or we do all of our work and try to get something back that we could have had if we hadn't beat it out of each other . . .

I think that my perceptions of life are less negative and angry. I don't assign the negativity. For example, I look back and feel a lot more compassion for my family than I did when I was growing up being angry that my father was an alcoholic and feeling my mother should have jettisoned him and gone out and gotten a job and everything would have been all right. I understand better where they came from. So I understand better how influences on children affect the damage and what we have to overcome to make it in the world and how there's not enough support for the positive. I understand that better now, so I have more compassion. I also feel more responsibility to young people and more responsibility to make a difference.

Chapter 12

The Belief in You

Somebody asked me a favorite saying, and this is something I always write on my pictures to kids, or tell them: "Your achievements can be as great as your dreams." And that's true of anybody of any age. There are no closed doors, to anyone.

Nancy Currie

Perhaps more than any other chapter, this one expresses the philosophy behind this book. I asked these women what advice or ideas they would like to share with other women who want to live their dreams, as they themselves have done. In response, these outstanding, remarkable women offer the very essence of their beliefs.

We are all in the process of becoming, and we can learn so much from other women. Please read these words, learn from them, and reflect upon their messages. Be touched by them, and perhaps you will awaken new possibilities for yourself.

Isabel Allende

Author

It's so difficult for me to give any advice, because lives are all so different. I think that each one of us has her journey, her own road to travel, and we all have different talents and strengths that are different. The only cure I know for my obsessions and my losses is writing. But that's not the case with everybody. Other people do it other ways, so it's very hard to give any sort of advice.

The only thing I would recommend to every woman is to get together with other women, because there is a sisterhood out there. When we were young and we were in our reproductive stage, we often forgot about that sisterhood. We were so hooked into the sexual partnership. We were so hooked with men and in the stage of attracting men and sharing with men that we forgot the time when we were little and we had friends, the time when we were children and we had our mothers. We forgot our sisters. There's great strength and wisdom that we can obtain from other women who are going through the same things that we are. That's why I think that a book like this is important. It allows us to get in touch with other stories, the stories of other women, and realize how much we have in common and how differently people cope with similar situations so that we can find in ourselves, and in them, ways to cope, ways to change.

Comfort. Joy. Laughter. Humor. I think that one of the extraordinary things that women have is that they laugh and cry so easily together. What is, unfortunately, so hard for men, we woman share automatically. Sometimes I meet people I have never seen before, and in less than five minutes we're crying together. And it's not embarrassing at all. We learn from that laughter and sharing of tears. It's very comforting.

Whenever I confront any situation in life I ask myself the question, "What is the most generous and loving thing to do?" And usually that helps me in my decision. I learned something when Paula died and I thought that I had lost everything. I had lost even her physical presence. She was just a corpse when they took her away. I entered into a sort of void. All the effort I had done to keep her alive was gone. There was nothing to do except to sit there, sit in that empty room. When everything was lost and done, I realized that I had the love I had given her. She could not give back that love at the time, because she couldn't give back anything. But it didn't matter. The love that I gave her, that was the treasure I had.

By extension, the only thing I own is what I give. The only thing I have is what I give in every aspect of life. When I give away my book, when I publish it and other people own it, then it's my book. Before, it's nothing. It's a bunch of papers on a table. It's not even a book. It becomes the book when you give it away.

When do you become a grandmother? When you give your love and the dedication of your time to the grandchildren. It's not an abstract term. It becomes something when you give; before you give, it's nothing. When does food becomes a meal? When you give it, when you share it; before, it's just ingredients, not a meal. When does love become love? When you share it with somebody else. It's not an abstract feeling. You don't go around like St. Francis loving in the abstract, you love in a very concrete and practical way. You love by doing things for somebody, or for some cause. I think that that is the only thing I have.

When I had to let go of Paula's body, she was wrapped in a sheet. I put some warm socks on her feet and the portraits of my grandchildren and myself in her hands, and that was it. She couldn't take anything with her. She left as she came, totally naked. She didn't own anything. So all these things that you see here can be destroyed or be stolen or burnt tomorrow, and I don't care because they don't mean anything. I will be like my daughter in a sheet, and it's wonderful. Isn't that wonderful? It's very simple and very comforting.

Lynn Woolsey

Congresswoman

I truly believe in women. A young woman said to me the other day, "That was really fun. I usually don't enjoy being around a bunch of women." I said, "That's because you're young. You're going to learn that that's where you get most of the power and most of the feedback you need for your life, from other women. Old, young, all around you. Depend on other women. Let women be your friends. Nothing is more important than your women friends."

First of all, if we don't compete, we understand each other. Men are so competitive, and women have a whole different set of egos. I hope we don't learn to have male egos as we get more and more. That's why women are important to each other. They can talk about things that are so important to them. Some men, yes, but most can't relate to our stuff.

My major thing I tell young people is, if you're interested, get involved. Do it in pieces. Don't think you have to do it all at once. Don't take on more than you can take care of. If you're interested in something—yourself first, I hope—then be involved. Take charge. Don't let the world do it to you. Take charge of your piece of you and particularly yourself. Care about yourself enough to take care of yourself.

Carmel Greenwood

Entrepreneur

I would say change your life, have courage, and don't let anyone or anything stand in your way. You can change in five seconds, you can change who you are, what you believe in. You can change the people around you. When you change, everything in your life changes.

That was my major discovery: I didn't have to change everybody, all I had to change was myself. I realized that you may leave people behind, but your situation could change in five seconds if you change your beliefs about who you are. Then your situation changes. And you have to be willing to let go. I've let go of many people in my life. Now, if I'm with somebody, I really tune into whether I get a charge from them or whether I'm drained. If I'm drained, I don't see them again . . . [Laughter]

There are only two things, fear or love. So when you're feeling very fearful, replace it with love. Love dissolves all fear. Love dissolves all negative thoughts.

In my healing work, people get very sick because of blocked fear. It might be something that happened when they were children, but it actually gets stuck in the body. It might be in the heart. A lot of women, it's in the heart. When I see a person, I can see right through the body. I get a picture of what happened to them, and I can actually move the energy out and heal the person. It might be arthritis, heart problem, walking pneumonia, and all of it is blocked fear that gets stuck in the body. So the object is to keep it moving through the body. When you bring in the liquid gold from the universe, it just moves right through the body, so you're flowing all the time, you have incredible life force.

People who look like worn-out shells, it's because their life force is gone; they've compromised. If you're in a marriage that is bad and you're compromising, you'll end up a shell. It's not worth it.

You know, it's not a dress rehearsal. Have fun and enjoy it!

Gretchen Dewitt
Public relations professional

So, life is a surprise and there will be good surprises, things that we never conceived. We think that we've thought about everything we ever want to do, and then we discover, "Here's something that I never even thought about that's happening to me."

Love. Love. I think that's what we have to do is to love, and if we love we will be loved back. It's very mathematical, it's like any mathematical equation, it's like looking in a mirror. If we look at someone and love them, we will be loved back.

I am very happy that I was born, and extremely pleased that I am here on earth, and the message is, women really are in charge of life, and that's an important responsibility, and the most wonderful thing anybody can be doing. It's really us who keep the human race going. We don't go to war fighting over territories or gold; we never really have. We're the ones who really decide who's going to be born and when, and women can be anything they want to be.

I love the letter of Paul on faith, hope, and charity, which is love. This influenced my life the most at difficult and happy times, the idea that love endures. It's the strongest emotion. So when there is grief, that grief will subside, but love is stronger than grief. It lives the longest. It never dies. So when Paul talked about languages dying, that knowledge would be replaced, it's all true. When he was speaking, he was speaking in Greek or Latin; those languages are dead languages. So, languages are dead, but knowledge is constantly being replaced. Science always has something new, there's a new spin on what we think is fact.

What really lives, what endures, is love. That is the most important message I've gotten in my life. So when I've had terrible times or difficult times, I know that love will be the strongest emotion.

We are surrounded by friends who lose people. Whether they're eighty-two or two, people leave this life, and it's important to remember that love is the emotion we will be left with. A gratitude for the life of that particular person. And that feeling will outlive the feelings of sorrow for having been left behind.

Alice Waters
Restaurateur/Author/Educator

Well, it's not about money. It's really not. Doing this work was never about money, and I was lucky that people came. But I think that's what happens when you do something that you're passionate about—the money follows.

I've always thought, when I lose my passion here, I'll close the restaurant. And I still feel that way. I will. And you have to be ready to do that, because that's what it's about.

Madeleine Albright
Former Secretary of State

What I would say to women is this. Today it is more important than ever to know what is happening around you, so take the time to learn about our world. Study a foreign language, if you can, and follow current events. Begin by reading a daily newspaper, or one of the weekly news magazines.

You will find that the solution to every problem begins with one person taking action. Wherever I went to school, I would start an International Relations Club (because I started it, I would become president!).

It is sad but true that there are not enough women holding jobs in foreign affairs. At the UN, I was one of six female permanent representatives. The other 179 were men. Correcting this is not simply about fairness. Today's world needs the skills and experience that women bring to diplomacy. So I encourage you to get involved—we need you.

There are also growing international business opportunities. Most importantly, set your sights as high as possible and pursue every opportunity.

I also think it is only a matter of time before we have a woman President of the United States.

Rosie Casals

Professional athlete

My feeling is that it's so hard to know what it is you want to do. That's half the challenge. Going through life trying to figure out what you want to be, who you want to be, and what you want to do. So, don't be afraid to take chances, don't be afraid to pursue your dreams, the things that you think that are important to you. If you make a mistake, you make a mistake. That's life. And you learn from your mistakes. That's important. You've got to learn from your mistakes. You've got to learn how to approach things so that they work for you rather than the other way. It's like playing a match. If you make the same mistakes, you keep losing. You must be smarter than that. You must pay attention. I think if you pay attention to the things that are going to make a difference in your life, you will have a pretty good life.

Be true to yourself. Don't be afraid to follow your dreams. It's so easy for people to say, "You're not going to do that! Are you crazy?" You know, I'm a little bit crazy, because I think that's what keeps people going. Some people like the same thing. Other people need changes. But somewhere along the line, you get to a point in your life where you need a change. And you can't be afraid. You can't be afraid to make a change. When you get to a point when you are looking at something different because you feel that you need to have that, then go ahead. Go for it.

Leslie Young
Ballet soloist

I remember when the ballet was on tour in Hawaii once, and we were given a membership to one of those workout clubs just for the time we were there. I was there late, and I guess I had a pearl necklace on, and there was a lady who was cleaning up. And she said, "Oh, I don't like pearls." She was gathering towels, and for some reason I decided to stop and say, "But I *like* pearls." And she said, "Why?" It was just a weird passing moment, and I said, "Well, because a pearl is something that started out as an irritation and was made really beautiful with time and care. It's a beautiful thing." And she looked at me with this incredible look of openness. It didn't seem like anything to me until I saw her look, and then I realized I had made a difference.

I have three quotes to share. "No love, no friendship can cross the path of our destiny without leaving some mark on it forever." François Marquois says this one. St. Francis of Assisi says, "Go out and preach the gospel, and if you have to, use words." I love that saying because it's about the little things you do and about challenging you to find a different way to speak. And then there is one that I recently gave to a friend that says, "Be like a duck . . . calm on the surface and paddling like the dickens underneath."

Elizabeth Colton
Entrepreneur

If you believe in who you are, it's almost enough to keep going. I think the real question is, how do you get to that place where you do believe in yourself so that you can keep going? You have to find the inspiration from around you—be it your children, the women from the past, your mother—you have to find that inspiration. Maybe it's your best friend; whatever it is to help you get to the place where you believe in yourself.

If you come from a family or live in a community where it's hard to make ends meet and feed yourself and your family, it's a lot harder to believe in yourself. I understand that. But recently I read this story in the paper about these women in India who had nothing and got together and started their own bank with pennies to support their own local businesses. They've gone from nothing to supporting themselves and others to have some kind of a meaningful existence. There are a lot of inspiring stories around from that kind of situation.

My mother really had nothing to worry about economically, but she couldn't believe in herself because she wasn't allowed to. If she had taken some other road, found a group of women . . . Maybe in her time there wasn't any support available. One of the advances we've made is that there's a lot of support available now. If you want and need to find it, it's out there, be it professional groups or book groups or whatever it is. There's a lot of support for women if you can find it.

I'll tell you a story that is sort of an aside. My brother is six years older than I am and quite conservative, I think, socially and politically. I sent him a newspaper article about one of the projects this museum had done, and in it there was a quote from me. It said, "If we want men to value women as equals in the future and women to see themselves as equals, then we must present equal images from the past." As a gift to me, he took that quote from the newspaper article and had it written in calligraphy and designed and decorated and framed, and he sent it to me. To think that my own brother, who I would think would have no consciousness about women's issues, would feel strongly enough to recognize and believe in what I had said—that was one of those moments of incredible encouragement that you asked about earlier. That quote he had framed is up on my wall, and it still brings me courage sometimes to believe in myself and this project.

Annelies Atchley
Educator/Artist

You can't believe in yourself if you don't get to know the other person. You have no self without a mirror. If you want to know how good or how bad or how wonderful you are, serve. Go to an old age home and serve. Go to a zoo and serve. Serve the environment . . .

I think if you want something out of life, you have to look at yourself and say, "Do I give this thing I want? Do I give freedom to this person when I want my own freedom? Do I give the love?"

Get spiritual. I think that the connection to nature and earth and your connectedness to your basic nature is the most important. If you know that you're a mammal and that you're in nature and that you're part of nature and that you can't live without nature and that you're like a mouse running around in your little environment, I think that will change you, first of all. Second, it will give you the peace and the excitement and the depth and beauty that nature has, and it will teach you how to fight and survive. Nature can be very tough and very rough and very unforgiving. On the other hand, it can be very forgiving and very nurturing. If you live every moment of your life to take care of the earth and to take care of something, you will live a rich life.

Laurel Burch
Artist

I think the most profound way that I've ever experienced believing in myself came from listening to my own heart and not measuring myself to others but really being the best that I can be. I would want to say to other women that I want them to know that that's a voice inside of you. So often you see people looking outside of themselves for strength or truth or wisdom or guidance. I just have this strong sense that a lot of my own well-being and success—I'm not talking about the big business success, but I mean in terms of being a successful human being—comes from being successful on my own terms and in my own ways and according to my beliefs and values. I think that that's inside of all of us, so my tendency in wanting to inspire other women has to do with that. I always think more about looking inside of yourself and being comfortable with who you are and being the best that you can be in your world and on your terms. Somehow I think that's been such a guiding light for me.

What life messages can change lives? That question just brings a fire in me. I am such a believer in change, and I wish I could take some of my own courage and just sprinkle it on the heads of other women. I think one of the most important things is first of all to express it. Things can become real when they're expressed and articulated, in the same way that my art and my feeling has an existence when I put it on paper. In the same way, when someone has a sense that they want to make a change, or cause a change, it's important to find a safe place to do that, whether it's with yourself or with friends or family, whatever. Articulate and express it and let it take shape. It takes courage to even say it out loud, because there's such a fear about change. Sometimes you hold it inside of you and try and figure it all out and think, "Well, when I get all dressed, when I have all the trappings and I have this all figured out, then I will do this." I think that any time I ever put it out in the world, the rest followed somehow.

I think you have to invite change. You have to welcome it with all its mystery and all the things that make it exciting. But to articulate it and to share it and express it, I think, is very, very important.

Sue Backman

Entrepreneur/Billiards professional

Anything is possible. I don't speak just from my personal experience but also from the experience of people I know. I think that if you really believe in yourself and believe that you can create your own reality, you will. But you must have total belief, and you must give yourself the opportunity to succeed. It's never too late, and each person has unlimited potential. I think if you operate from that you can create your life in such a way that you will be happy and fulfilled.

"Whatever doesn't kill me makes me stronger." I keep going back to that. I collect quotes. I write them down in my little pile that I have. I have little slips of paper, and I just love great quotes. But I think that one is pretty key for me. I have to remind myself that I think of myself as being a survivor and a person who is capable of having my life evolve in such a way that it will just get better and better. Even though sometimes things come up that block my path, I just have to find ways of stepping around them or jumping over them or building another road somewhere else if I have to. I've never come up against anything that I couldn't survive or get past.

There are two things we haven't touched upon that I think are key. One of them is the idea of operating in a man's world and not being afraid to do that. Just make your road.

I also think of myself as being a bridge builder, always trying to get people together and see what they have in common and how they can help each other. I think that approach has started to take hold a little more in the last couple of years. When I came into the industry nineteen years ago, everybody had their pieces of turf, and nobody wanted to share anything. They were all afraid of each other. Operating out of fear. It's just a bad way to go.

There has been a lot of talk in recent years about the goddess and goddess mythology, and is God a woman or man or whatever. What I have come to believe is that all of the problems in the world stem from the denial of the feminine and denial of the goddess, if you want to say that, or of that aspect of God that is loving and emotional. When I think of God, I think of God in four parts: I think of the father, the son who came to the earth as Jesus Christ for a period of time, the holy spirit, and the mother of everything who embodied herself in Mother Earth. If we are ever to get past all the problems that we see on earth—everything from pollution to abuse of other humans and animals—it all boils down to respect for the mother of everything and for the life on this earth. Unless everybody understands or gets that we are all part of the same thing, that there's a true sacredness to life, we will never survive. The survival of humankind is tied into coming to love and accept all life. I'm not a radical vegetarian or anything like that; it's more just respect. It boils down to respect for everyone, for other human beings, for other animals, and for the earth itself.

Nancy Currie

Astronaut

Somebody asked me a favorite saying, and this is something I always write on my pictures to kids, or tell them: "Your achievements can be as great as your dreams." And that's true of anybody of any age. There are no closed doors, to anyone. It's up to you to try as hard as you can to succeed in whatever you want, whether it's being the best architect, or greatest artist, or an astronaut. Anything that you want to do is achievable, if you're able to put forth the perseverance and the effort necessary, because many things won't come easily. If they came easily they probably wouldn't be so rewarding. Anything great usually requires a certain level of effort to achieve.

I speak from experience. I was a single parent, going to school at night, getting my PhD, while I was in this job. At some point I thought, "Why am I even doing this?" And I did it because there's going to come a time when I'm too old to do this job anymore, and I wanted to be able to go back and teach those folks that could then come in and do this job that I've enjoyed so much. I felt I could help them gain all the qualifications. And so it was worth staying up all night and going to school at night to finish up a PhD while being a single parent and working.

Anything is achievable. It may not be fun, and you may have to shift your priorities for a while. Obviously, for example, there wasn't time for me to date for a while. When you're a single mom and you're going to school and you're an astronaut, there isn't a whole lot of extra time. But you do what you can. If it's something that you really want to do, it's achievable. Your achievements truly can be as great as your dreams.

Rabbi Stacy Friedman
Rabbi

First of all, I think that it's an ever increasingly wonderful time to be a woman today. Think about what it would have been like to live in a time when a woman couldn't have a home or own property. I think that so many doors are open to women today. Just think about the fact that the girls in school today who are learning and studying can do anything because there are few doors closed to them.

On the other hand, there are also so many things that get in the way of women, like Madison Avenue and all those magazines, because we're supposed to look like a certain thing or act like a certain thing. So I think the most important thing is to try to get in touch with the best that God puts within us and that voice that God has put within us. We call it the holiness within us. Each person lives with a spark of the divine within, and I think it's important to find that. If you find that at whatever age, you can't get lost. If you know what that spark of divinity is within you, then you know that no matter what color your hair is or who your boyfriend is or whatever, you've got a gift for playing violin or you've got a gift of caring for babies or you can speak really well, or whatever it might be. Get in touch with what that spark of divinity is, and put yourself in situations or be around people who help to fan that flame and make it brighter, not around people who try to put it out.

That's probably the most important, but in addition to that, do not be afraid to stand on your own and to meet other people both ways. I think in the eighties we got the idea that we had to be really independent. Independence is very important, but dependency is very important also. So balance that . . .

One quote that I like and try to live by is from the Psalms: "This is the day that God has made; let us be happy and rejoice in it." For me that means that today is the day that we have, and it's a gift from God and an opportunity for us. For me it means to keep in the present, as opposed to living tomorrow or next week or next year or worrying what am I going to do and all of those things. It means remembering that this is what I have right here, and this is a gift from God and to try to live in the present and to make the most of it.

Valerie Coleman Morris
Anchorwoman/TV personality

Treat people the way you want to be treated. If people show you who they are, believe them the first time. Don't believe you can fix everything for everybody. Be larger than the moment or the crisis. Be as proactive as you can be rather than reactive. Choose your friends wisely. Remember to be kind to other women because each of us, I believe, is in the midst of some battle. Not necessarily a war, but these skirmishes and battles along the way. Just be kind to women.

Sylvia Boorstein
Author/Educator/Lecturer

What do women need to believe in themselves? I think, first of all, that everybody should believe in themselves and not just women. Up until now it's been really necessary to ask this question because in a world where women were not so favored and equally encouraged with men, it's really been for many women an uphill struggle to make their place. I'm hopeful that in the next generation from now the question will be what everybody needs to believe in themselves.

I think that as we catch on as parents and teachers and community people, we learn how valuable it is to be encouraging everybody to be just exactly like they are. There's that line in "Home on the Range" where they say, "where never is heard a discouraging word." I said before that one of the wonderful things about my parents was that they never told me a bad word. I'm sure they taught me how to behave myself, because I behaved myself very well. But they never told me a bad word. They never told me I wasn't doing right, and I wasn't any kind of a goody two-shoes. Sometimes I didn't do my homework, and I didn't always practice the violin, and I did sneak cigarettes. I waited until I was around the corner and I put on the lipstick and I went to school. So I didn't always behave exactly the way they wanted me to, but they told me what they needed for me to get that they loved me. And for the most part I never did anything that was a bad thing to do. I think that's what everybody needs, to know they are valued just as them . . .

Life is manageable. It's a feasible thing to do a life. You can do it honestly. Everybody's life is challenged. Who doesn't have health problems, mother problems, father problems, relationship problems, children problems? Everybody has problems. However, be able to manifest in your life that we can do this, we can live a life inevitably challenged and we can do it with kindness, compassion, humor, and beauty. Each of us walking around in a life manifesting this is like a mindfulness bell for everybody else: Hey! A life is possible. I'm thrilled to have spiritual teachers who don't do anything extraordinary. Their lives are as complicated as mine, but they're living them.

I said before that when we're not frightened or confused or over-whelmed or clouded with some mind state that's taken over our ability to see clearly, then we are quite naturally loving and generous and thoughtful and aware of other people and eager to make other people comfortable. We don't have to be given friendliness lessons in life or compassion lessons in life. We are naturally compassionate when we see people suffering. If our own hearts are at ease, what we naturally do is take care of other people. I think that's our purpose in life: to be able to discover our ways to stay at ease and feel ourselves and feel at home in our lives and be delighted to be alive in our lives so that we can look around and take care of the people around us.

The line that really inspires me is the line of a prayer: "Purify my heart so that I may truly serve." That's the line that inspires me.

Reverend Veronica Goines

Presbyterian pastor

I think believing in ourselves is a process, and it takes us time to get there . . .

I think I can't talk about this without getting into my religious beliefs. I strive to teach that God desires and wills to be connected with each one of us. We have to be able to maintain that. For me, it needs to be the place that I operate from. My centering is in Jesus. That is the relationship that is so crucial to my life. When I find myself beginning to be more concerned about all the externals—whether it's people or things—then I lose my centering and my peace, and I really can't do anything for anybody. So I have to regain that, and that I can only do through prayer.

I do need to take time out to be in prayer, but also just to do some self-care. Sometimes it's even physical. I'll get out and do a six-mile walk. When I go to the gym, that's time that is just rebuilding and recharging me. But prayer is certainly another of those ways. That can be almost anywhere that I can pray. Also just getting myself centered and recognizing what it is that's really bugging or bothering me and owning it and confessing it and saying to Jesus when I talk to him, "Lord, this is really, really bugging me. This is really making me angry." I try to name it so that I can leave it there when I pray and I can gain a renewed perspective and get myself refocused so that I can leave not feeling victimized or diminished but empowered and able to make some clear decisions or changes.

Sometimes it's confronting people personally. Sometimes people are less willing to come to me if they have a problem and find it easier to take potshots in sniper wars and things like that. There are times that I have to go back and get myself centered and go to that person and be able to confront them. They're not able to do it, or aren't willing, or whatever it is, but it's not okay for me to let it go and just bug me or allow resentment to build up. I need to deal with it so that I'm clear enough to live and deal with everything else I need to do and be . . .

My calling is really a life calling. Years ago a friend of mine said, "I want to be a person who follows Christ and not a person who follows people who follow Christ." That has continued to be what guides my life. I really choose to have a direct relationship and connection and faith life that I continue in terms of my own disciplines so that I'm guided internally and inwardly. I'm informed externally, but not guided externally. That's what I strive to teach to my own members, to empower people to make the decision to live out of their own faith life.

Irene Zisblatt Zeigelstein
Holocaust survivor

I would advise every woman, young and old, whether they have a young family or a grown family, to appreciate every single day and especially with their families, because everything else is replaceable, but you cannot replace your family. People take it for granted that it's always going to be there or it's always going to be like that, but we know different . . .

Talking about a soul, I'll give you an experience about my soul. In the concentration camp, on Simchat Torah they decided to give us a concert because it was a happy holiday. After staying in roll call for about five hours in the mud, we couldn't wait to get back into the barrack. They chased us out again, and we were out in front of the camp. The crematoriums were burning, the ashes were falling like snow, and we were sitting in the hot ashes and a group of young inmates marched up on a podium where women and men SS were sitting in beautiful, clean, crisp clothes and lipstick and perfume and all that. And the concentration camp band came up, and they were playing, and they were ordered to play melodies to the heart, not to the soul. Thirty-two thousand women sitting, listening to this music and watching these SS women and men looking so beautiful, and we were covered with mud and lice and dirt and no hair and a piece of clothing, and the six crematoriums were making ashes out of our future children, and they were playing music to the heart, not to the soul.

After four or five hours, they let us go back inside. And as we were walking back inside, I fell in the mud, and I couldn't get up. I had been sitting in the hot ashes, and I guess my legs just gave out, and I couldn't get up. And as I was sitting in the mud, I thought, "What do they want from me? Why don't they tell me? Why do they make me suffer like this? They already took my parents, they took my siblings, they took my possessions, they shaved my hair, they took my name, they branded me with a number that represents a nothing. What do I have that they want before they kill me?" The only think I could think of was my soul. And I sat there and I looked on my legs and I couldn't move my legs and I was all full of mud and I got very angry and I said, "Well, they're not going to get my soul." And I picked myself up from the mud and I stood up and I walked into the barrack and I started to fight for my life, and I've been fighting ever since. And that came from the soul.

No one can take my soul. And nobody did. I think that was part of my strength that helped me survive. It has made me be happy to be here every single minute of my life.

I have no hatred in my life. People ask me, "How much do you hate the Germans?" I do not hate the Germans. I feel sad about it, I feel angry about it, but I have no hatred in my life. I am just very, very happy. I do not complain about not having a Mercedes. I wouldn't ride in it anyway even if I would have it. I don't feel that any material thing is important in my life. I never did anything aggressive like hurting anybody to become rich. I would never even think of anything like that, like being in competition. You know how they say, "It's a dog-eat-dog world, you've got to look out for yourself"? I was always the last one I looked out for. It was always the other guy first. And I got hurt many a time, but that was okay. It didn't bother me.

The most important thing in my life is human beings. Children especially. There is nothing in the world that I am asked to do that concerns children that if it's in my power I would refuse. That's my priority in life.

My friends say, "Aren't you ever complaining about anything?" I just know I have nothing to complain about. It's okay with me. What can happen? What's the worst that can happen?

Marti McMahon
Entrepreneur

I would say, find your passion and absolutely go for it. Don't be afraid to ask for help. Be willing to take the risk. Don't just be in a situation that you're not challenged, that you're not going to grow. Stretch yourself and keep those eyes open to all these opportunities around you, and just go for it.

Sit down, meditate, and see whether you really are happy in what you are doing right at this point. Also look and see where you want to be five years from now, ten years from now. Look into the future and see where you want to be. And if you're not doing what you want to be doing and you realize that what you're doing now isn't going to guide you or help you accomplish what you want to accomplish five or ten years from now, then change course, go in a different direction.

Make the most of your time here and touch people in any way that you can in your life. I'm a real people person and being able to make that difference has made me feel very fulfilled and happy. It may not be so for people who are more introverted. Perhaps their direction is completely someplace else. Like a scientist, maybe doing research in something that is going to be better for the world would be their way of reaching out to people. I'm a touchy, feely person. I have to have them around me.

Be passionate, and when you see someone without a smile, give them one of yours, and just watch those smiles grow.

Mary Bitterman
President/CEO, public television

I've never felt that I should presume to give advice. Everyone's life is so different. I guess one can only say that in living her own life, certain things have been meaningful and helpful, and that others may want to think about those little messages and see if they work for them.

But I think if anybody wants to change her life, it's usually to change it toward greater satisfaction, self-fulfillment, and a sense of well-being, a sense of pride. To do that, I think, requires the basic values that we talked about at the very start of the conversation—to be true to yourself and to others.

Sometimes some women become very unhappy because they've been raised in such a way, or they've been given to circumstances where they become extremely punitive on themselves. Everything that goes wrong is their fault. They brood over this, they become unhappy, they oftentimes become unwell. I'm not one of these people involved in all of these health things and wellness things; I can only tell you from my own personal experience that happier people seem to be healthier people.

People sometimes worry about what in Hawaii we call menini things, little, tiny, nothing things. Before you get unhappy or hysterical or upset or whatever, analyze the situation and see if this is really worth getting upset about. It may be that this is just a kind of annoyance. It may be that the more you think about it, you're going to realize that some idiot saying something idiotic just is not the substance on which you want to lose a night's sleep. You put these things into perspective.

I think, too, of having an appropriate sense of women's abilities and being humble, in the real, true definition of that word, which means being truthful. If someone is a great athlete, it would not be humble for him to say, "I'm really a lousy athlete." That would be dishonest. But to be humble is to be pretty clear with yourself about who you are and to have a sense of knowing who you are, where you came from, and who has made your progress possible. I think that gives you a good footing for having some control over your life and being able to manage it in a direction that is congenial to your values and to your sense of purpose.

Again, I think my favorite quote is Goethe's, that no matter how difficult things become, it is that great characteristic of humanity to live on hope. There are too many circumstance in history, recent as well as long past, in which things have been so incredibly difficult. There are times in people's lives where there is just such tremendous sadness. And yet there's that sort of irrepressibility of being hopeful. If the

Kosovar refugees right now did not have some sense of hope, they would shoot themselves rather than wait to be shot. It's that irrepressible human dimension of an ability to live on hope that I think really keeps everyone going.

And there's that wonderful statement of Socrates, who said that the wise man never becomes overly upset when things go badly, because all things change; and the wise man never becomes euphoric when things go well, because all things change. We need to recognize that life is going to have its ups and its downs, and that the important thing is to so appreciate those good times, those precious moments, those moments of happiness. They give you the strength to walk through the valley of tears. They give you the strength to be able to rebound after even a fairly sustained period of enormous difficulty and disquiet. These happy moments of one's life can be very unremarkable in terms of a larger world, but my own view is the very positive strength that you take from those happy moments is what keeps you going during the distress times.

Jeanne Rizzo

Entrepreneur

If you want to change your life, first sit with your life and know it. Come to know your heart and your soul and find what pleases you.

It's back to the idea of intuition and pleasure. I honestly believe that when women follow what pleases them, they make incredible contributions. We need to honor that, to honor what pleases us as women and not the paradigm that we're called upon to respond to all the time about what pleases men and others. If it pleases you to be at home when your kids get home from school, then be at home when your kids get home and find a way to do that. But understand that it's pleasing you, that you're not meeting some obligation, that you suspend the rules and sit with yourself and understand who you are on this earth, and you ask, how do you want to travel through it? What do you want to be able to say if you have one year to live? What are the practices that you would practice in that year? What would you do? Forgive whom you need to forgive, seek forgiveness where you need to seek it and find the things that you would do if this was the last year of your life and you knew it was. How would you live it? Then live your life that way.

I'm going to go back to the June Jordan poem that Sweet Honey in the Rock turned into a song: "We are the ones, we are the ones we've been waiting for." I think it's about us, it's about waiting for ourselves and knowing that we're waiting for ourselves. And as women we are the only ones that we can wait for. We are the ones who are going to make the difference. I think about that and carry that with me, whether it's a political movement, whether it's how I deal in my own home, in my love life, in my art . . . If I don't pull out the drum set and start playing drums, I'm the only one that can do that, so I'm waiting for myself. I think that's what guides me: waiting for myself.

Contributors

Madeleine Korbel Albright is former Secretary of State of the United States. She was the first female Secretary of State and the highest-ranking woman in the history of the U.S. government. As a Research Professor of International Affairs and Director of Women in Foreign Service Program at Georgetown University's School of Foreign Service, she has taught undergraduate and graduate courses in international affairs, U.S. foreign policy, Russian foreign policy, and Central and Eastern European politics, and she is responsible for developing and implementing programs designed to enhance women's professional opportunities in international affairs. Awarded a BA with honors in political science from Wellesley College, she studied at the School of Advanced International Studies at Johns Hopkins University. She received a Certificate from the Russian Institute at Columbia University, and her master's degree and doctorate from Columbia University's Department of Public Law and Government.

Isabel Allende, born in Peru, is an internationally acclaimed author who was raised in Chile, worked as a journalist for many years, and began writing fiction in 1981. Since then her books have been translated into twenty-seven languages, and two of them were made into motion pictures and theater plays. All of her works have a common theme: Life is precious and should be free from oppression. Her novels feature female protagonists whose strength, intelligence, and creativity enable them to endure hardships, fight oppression, and improve the world around them. She went into exile after her uncle, Chilean president Salvador Allende, was overthrown and killed in a CIA-assisted coup in 1973. Her books include the international best-seller *The House of the Spirits, Aphrodite: A Memoir of the Senses, Of Love and Shadows, Eva Luna, The Stories of Eva Luna, Infinite Plan, Paula, Daughter of Fortune,* and *Portrait in Sepia.*

Annelies Atchley, born in Switzerland, struggled to survive as an immigrant to the United States. She was a kindergarten teacher in the Reed Union School District, Tiburon, California, for many years. Presently she teaches art to children of all ages from a studio in her home.

Sue Backman is ranked among the top billiards players in America and is a member of the women's professional tour. She is co-owner of the upscale Chalkers billiards clubs in San Francisco and Emeryville, California, and has served as President of the Emeryville Chamber of Commerce and the local Leukemia Society.

Mary G. F. Bitterman, PhD, is President and CEO of public television station KQED in San Francisco, California. A former Director of Voice of America, she serves on the Board of Directors for twelve companies and organizations, including The World Affairs Council; Bay Area Council; Association of America's Public Television; Bank of Hawaii; National Academy of Public Administration; Pacific Forum/CSIS; and Project Dana of the Buddhist Churches of Hawaii. She has served as U.S. delegate to the United Nations Conference on Women, Copenhagen, 1980 Women of Vision Award, Career Action Center Silicon Valley 2000, Woman of the Year, American Women in Radio and Television (Northern California Chapter) 2001.

Sylvia Boorstein is an author and founding teacher of Spirit Rock Meditation Center in Woodacre, California, and a senior teacher at Insight Meditation Center in Barre, Massachusetts. She earned her doctorate in psychology in 1974. She lectures and teaches widely on the subject of mindfulness meditation and Judaism. She is the author of several books on mindfulness meditation, including *It's Easier Than You Think: The Buddhist Way to Happiness; Don't Just Do Something, Sit There: A Mindfulness Retreat with Sylvia Boorstein;* and *That's Funny, You Don't Look Buddhist: On Being a Faithful Jew and a Passionate Buddhist.*

Laurel Burch began making jewelry in San Francisco's Haight-Ashbury district in the late sixties, selling her designs on the streets and in local galleries. This former flower child and self-taught painter is now an internationally famous artist and designer with a flourishing business. Her artistic vision speaks a common language understood by all: the language of the heart. She has established a passionate career that has spawned hundreds of mythical animals, ethereal birds, and figures that capture the soul of humanity.

Rosie Casals was an innovator in women's tennis. She and her contemporaries—she was Billy Jean King's doubles partner—paved the way for women to compete with men for tournament prizes and television audiences. She continues to be an advocate for women's tennis and for women in sports.

Elizabeth L. Colton is President of the International Museum of Women, the first and only international, multicultural, world-class museum of women's history. The museum will be a permanent exhibit chronicling the lives of courageous women throughout the world and throughout history. The projected time for completion is 2006.

Nancy Currie, PhD, is a NASA astronaut who has logged over 737 hours in space. The recipient of numerous special honors, she has logged 3,900 flying hours in a variety of rotary wing and fixed wing aircraft. She received a BA in biological science from Ohio State University, a masters of science degree in safety from the University of Southern California, and a doctorate in Industrial Engineering from the University of Houston. She is the mother of one daughter.

Gretchen Dewitt is a public relations professional, a producer of special events, and a philanthropist who works with charitable organizations. She grew up on a farm in the Midwest, then pursued an education in Switzerland. She presently lives in Sausalito, California, where she has made wonderful contributions to the community.

Phyllis Diller, comedienne, contributed the poem "My Prayer."

Rabbi Stacy Friedman decided to become a rabbi at the age of sixteen. She studied at Brandeis University and the Hebrew University of Jerusalem. Rabbi Friedman moved to Mill Valley, California, in 1993 and is presently the Associate Rabbi of Congregation Rodef Shalom. She has served on a variety of community boards, including the board of the Marin Interfaith Youth Outreach, Marin Interfaith Council, the Pacific Association of Reform Rabbis, and the Northern California Board of Rabbis, where she is currently vice president.

Reverend Veronica Goines follows a tradition of preaching women. While earning her Masters of Divinity degree from San Francisco Theological Seminary, she served as chaplain to incarcerated youth and to adults as a resident chaplain of Stanford University Hospital. Presently, Reverend Goines is the Pastor of St. Andrew Presbyterian Church of Marin City, California. She credits her family for her earliest spiritual formation, most especially the consistent religious beliefs of her mother.

Carmel Greenwood, born and educated in Australia, went to Hong Kong for a two-week vacation and stayed. From humble beginnings she created Fortune Financial Consultants, Ltd., and managed the personal portfolios of her clients. She is married with five children and founded Carmel Concepts to produce tapes and items with a spiritual message. She is the author of *Letting Go and Loving Life*.

Jo Hanson received her Masters in Fine Arts from San Francisco State University and an MA in Education from the University of Illinois. She is an artist whose work features environmental themes and the recipient of numerous awards. She has exhibited widely and teaches occasionally at the University of California at Berkeley, the California College of Arts and Crafts, and the Otis Art Institute in Los Angeles. She is an active lecturer and panelist on the subject of art and the environment. Her work is exhibited nationally in numerous public and private collections.

Marti McMahon, a native of El Salvador, grew up near the Great Lakes in Chicago, Illinois, where she first enjoyed cruising and entertaining friends with gourmet meals. She attended DePaul University and the University of Mexico. With her husband and three children, she moved to the San Francisco Bay Area and founded Pacific Marine Yachts, a charter and dining cruise company with four yachts that can carry over seven hundred passengers. The company has twenty-three full-time and sixty-five part-time employees and earns annual revenues of more than five million dollars.

Valerie Coleman Morris was one of the San Francisco Bay Area's first African-American reporters and anchorwomen in the 1970s and '80s. Known for her calm and cool authority under pressure, she is now a reporter and anchor on CNNfn, hosting the stock market news three days a week, hosting the "Personal Finance" show, and doing financial updates for the CNN networks. In addition to her interview, she contributed the text of the Hopi Prayer for this book.

Sister Mary Neill, OP, is the author of four books, a professor, a workshop director, a lecturer, and co-director of Inner Explorations. She holds a doctorate from the University of Strasbourg and teaches courses in religion, spirituality, and moral philosophy.

Jeanne Rizzo is owner of JR Productions, a film, concert, theater, event production, artist management, and books business. She was cofounder of the Great American Music Hall, a 450-seat club in which she helped produce over five thousand nights of entertainment with some of America's best-known entertainers, as well as fund-raising benefits for many nonprofit groups. She was chosen to receive The Breast Cancer Fund's 1999 Bella Abzug Advocacy Award. She created the documentary film and CD "Climb Against the Odds," also for the Breast Cancer Fund.

Alice Waters graduated from the University of California at Berkeley in 1967 with a degree in French Cultural Studies. She is the author of five best-selling cookbooks and founder of the world-renowned Chez Panisse restaurant in Berkeley, California. She gives time to students at Martin Luther King Junior High School, teaching children the vital relationship of food to their lives and provides assistance with San Francisco's Garden Project. She also lends knowledge and support to the Horticulture Project, a job training and market garden program for the San Francisco County Jail. She has been recognized internationally for her achievements with many awards.

Lynn Woolsey was elected to the House of Representatives in 1992 and has been continually reelected to office ever since. She represents California's Sixth Congressional District, which consists of Marin County and most of Sonoma County. She is the first person elected to Congress to have been a single mother on welfare. She graduated from the University of San Francisco with a BS in Human Resources and Organizational Behavior in 1981. She has brought her unique experience to Congress to advocate for quality and affordable childcare and healthcare, and for family-friendly economic policies. She is the mother of four grown children and currently lives in the city of Petaluma.

Leslie Young is a ballerina soloist at the San Francisco Ballet who has given highly acclaimed performances in *Romeo and Juliet, Swan Lake, Sleeping Beauty,* and many other ballets. She has been the recipient of many honors, including the Princess Grace Foundation Award.

Irene Zisblatt Zeigelstein, a Holocaust survivor, grew up in Hungary. Her incredible story of childhood horror and survival—told by her, on-camera—was featured in Steven Spielberg's film *The Last Days.* She is an internationally renowned speaker and teacher.